Introducing
Software Engineering

Neville J. Ford and Mark Woodroffe

Prentice Hall

New York   London   Toronto   Sydney   Tokyo · Singapore

First published 1994 by
Prentice Hall International (UK) Ltd
Campus 400, Maylands Avenue
Hemel Hempstead
Hertfordshire, HP2 7EZ
A division of
Simon & Schuster International Group

Printed and bound in Great Britain by
T. J. Press (Padstow) Ltd

Library of Congress Cataloging-in-Publication Data

Available from the publisher

British Library Cataloguing in Publication Data

A catalogue record for this book is available from
the British Library

ISBN: 0-13-063884-6

2 3 4 5   98 97 96 95

Contents

Preface

Who is this book for?

This book is intended to support an introductory course in software engineering. It is also suitable for self-study and as a guide to software engineering techniques for those already employed in the computing industry. The content of the book assumes some knowledge of programming, equivalent to an introductory course in a high-level language such as Pascal, Modula-2 or C. It would also be helpful for the reader to have some prior knowledge of systems analysis. The bibliography lists a variety of books on the subject of systems analysis and some suggestions of suitable reading matter on developing computer programs in high-level languages, which will assist you if you find you need more background information.

The material covered in the book is aimed at higher education courses in computing and is particularly targeted at those who do not have a mathematical background. This is an important feature, since the number of students of computer science and similar courses who do not have a strong mathematical background is large and increasing. Another approach to software engineering makes heavy use of mathematics. This is introduced in an appendix on *formal methods*.

In a book of this size we cannot hope to give an exhaustive account of software engineering. Indeed, there are several alternative methods of engineering software which are widely used. Our aim in this work is to give a clear and detailed introduction and a good overview of the issues involved. This will enable the reader to find other more detailed and technical works later which are appropriate to the particular needs and interests of the individual. Studying the contents of this book should make the more technical works easier to understand.

How should you read this book?

We have provided questions for you to attempt throughout this book and they take four different forms:

Self-test questions: these are straightforward short questions with a straightforward answer. They are intended for you to answer as you read the text, and do not require any written work. Self-test questions are there to help you make sure that you have understood the page or two which you have just read, and help you to check that you have not fallen asleep!

Exercises: these will require more thought and you will probably need to write your answer out on paper. Exercises are designed to test more detailed understanding of key issues.

Assignments: these are major pieces of work which may require investigation, research or significant thought. You should not necessarily expect to complete every assignment.

Computer-based exercises: these are exercises which require access to a suitable software package (for example, a CASE tool).

A practical or theoretical course?

One of the principal contentions of software engineering is that much of the software previously written was inadequately planned. Therefore the planning process is crucial to the work of the software engineer. The actual implementation of the new software on computer forms only a very small proportion of the total picture. It is therefore possible to undertake much of the work described in this volume without any access at all to computers.

On the other hand, the computer is an ideal design tool for engineers of all disciplines, and the software engineer is no exception. While we would caution against the tendency to start to write programs at the earliest opportunity, we do encourage you to make use of computer aided software engineering (CASE) tools if you have them available. These CASE tools are designed to assist you in the processes of software engineering.

Chapter 1

What is software engineering?

1.1 Introduction

Software engineering is a relatively new term, which is used to describe modern
methods for developing software. Traditionally, software was developed by computer programmers. Some programs were well designed and written and were
relatively bug-free. Other programs suffered from poor design, poor programming
techniques and the presence of bugs. The title *software engineering* marks a new
approach to software development methods.

1.2 Background

During the last 50 years or so, the number of applications for computers has grown
almost without bound. Each computer application, from the smallest machine running a computer game, a simple word-processing package or a text editor, to large
mainframe computers running the payroll for a multi-national company, has one
thing in common: each application must be developed. Conventionally, we tend to
think in terms of people *programming* the applications. In this sense, programming
means writing computer programs in a *high-level language* or in *assembly language*
or *machine code*. More recently applications have often been developed using more
sophisticated tools, such as *expert system shells, database programming languages*
and *configurable applications packages.*

This book is about methods which may be used by software developers to aid
the development process. Many of the tools and methods have been used for some
time, others are newer. Together, the use of the methods and tools, motivated
by the desire to write efficient programs in an efficient manner forms the basis for
software engineering.

1.3   A software engineer's task

The typical work of the software engineer is expressed in terms of the need to write a particular program or to develop a particular application. The work of the software engineer links closely with the work of systems analysts, whose task it is to determine what programs and applications actually need to be developed to suit a particular user.

As we shall see, both the tasks and the methods of systems analysts overlap those of the software engineer, and this interrelationship is explored more thoroughly in Chapters 3 and 4. For our present purposes, we shall assume that the software engineer is faced with the job of designing and implementing a computer-based system, whose purpose is predetermined.

1.4   The software engineer's approach

Having been given a particular item of software to develop, we may identify five principal stages in the software engineer's work. These stages are illustrated in Figure 1.1.

Inevitably over a period of time, systems need to be redeveloped and modernised, and software maintenance often leads to the specification of a new improved system. Considered in this way, the software development process becomes a cycle, known as the software life cycle. We shall discuss the stages in this life cycle in much more detail as we proceed through the book.

1.4.1   Requirements definition

The requirements definition is an important document for the software engineer, since it can form the basis of the agreement made with the employing organisation. It describes in some detail the scope of the project is to be undertaken, and allows both parties to be clear that they have a good understanding of what the completed project will accomplish.

The requirements definition may well be the outcome of the systems analysis phase in the software life cycle. It includes descriptions of the requirements of the new system listed separately as the *functional requirements* and the *non-functional requirements*.

Thus we are able to distinguish between the actual tasks which are to be performed by the new system (the functional requirements) and the manner and times in which these tasks will be performed (the non-functional requirements). Once the requirements definition is completed, the software engineer is ready to begin the task of designing the actual software to be implemented.

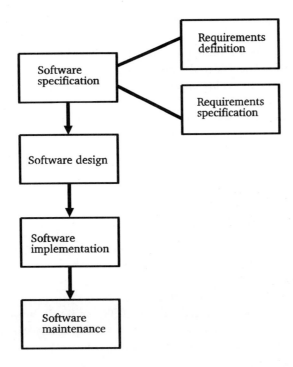

Figure 1.1 Stages in software engineering

1.4.2 Requirements specification

The requirements specification is a technical document in which the software engineer presents, in a formal way, the details of the system which is to be implemented. It requires a detailed analysis of the data types and structures to be employed in the implementation and a specification of the functions and procedures.

The main feature of a good requirements specification is that it should be clear, accurate and concise. Some software engineers rely upon the use of formal methods based upon discrete mathematics. In this book, we have taken the decision to discuss the ideas underlying the software specification in a relatively unmathematical way. However, Appendix I gives an indication of how formal methods can be used, how they can result in quality assurance benefits and the cost and difficulty involved in their use.

1.4.3 Software design

Once the *software specification* document, made up of the two subsections outlined above, is complete, the software engineer is able to move on to the design phase.

For many readers of the current text, some of the ideas underlying software design will be familiar.

Approaches to software design are frequently based upon a *top-down* method which allows for the successive decomposition of the problem under analysis into a series of subproblems. This approach is then repeated successively until each subproblem may be solved easily.

Alternative strategies (*bottom-up* design is one example) will also be discussed. These familiar techniques must be set alongside different methods, notably object-oriented design methods, which are based upon a rather different view of program design (see Appendix III).

1.4.4   Software implementation

From the design phase in the software development cycle, we move to the implementation, where the software is prepared for use on the system. Notable decisions have to be taken at this stage. The decision as to the *implementation medium* for the project is one of the most important.

This question will be addressed fully in Chapter 9. It involves the decision between the possibility of implementing a new system using existing applications packages or highly specialised software as an alternative to writing the programs in high-level language.

This is an issue sometimes neglected by software developers in general and by software engineers in particular. Software engineering, having grown out of computer programming, sometimes presupposes that the appropriate solution to a problem is based upon writing high-level code. This is not always the case.

Other issues are also important to us. Questions of program portability and maintainability are particularly significant here, since portable and easily maintainable code is less expensive to use in the long run. It is particularly to be hoped that programs designed methodically using software engineering techniques will be well written, comparatively easy to maintain and relatively bug-free.

1.4.5   Software maintenance

The discussion in the preceding subsection demonstrates the importance of software maintenance. In the late 1980s companies were spending as much as 80% of their entire software development budget on the maintenance and correction of previously written programs. If software is better designed and therefore more easily maintained, then there may be a cost saving in the long run!

1.4.6   Other issues

In the requirements definition, we identify functional and non-functional requirements as being important in the definition of the requirements for a new system.
It is all too easy to concentrate on the functional requirements during the implementational phase of the software engineering project, because the question of
whether the software will actually do the job or not governs the initial success of
the project.

However, over the longer term, the *quality* of the software in use will probably
be judged by the users more in terms of non-functional rather than functional
characteristics. Thus speed, ease of use and quality of the *user interface* become
important issues. This is our reason for including a section on software usabil-
ity, and software quality issues in general after the software implementation and
maintenance chapters.

1.5   What, then, is software engineering?

We return to our initial question. Software engineering provides a collection of
methods and techniques which may be employed within the software development
cycle. The use of these methods is designed to improve the software development
process by encouraging better design methodologies and thereby producing programs which are more easily maintained and contain fewer bugs. The software
engineer therefore plays the same role in the production of computer software as
the civil engineer plays in the construction of a new bridge; the engineer approves
the design, makes sure the methods to be used are appropriate, oversees and tests
the construction, checks up on the quality and advises on maintenance.

You could build a bridge without a civil engineer. You can write computer
programs without a software engineer. In either case, employing the expert who
uses the approved design methods will reduce your chance of disaster.

1.6   Exercises

Self-test questions

Do software engineers:

- interview clients?
- design programs?
- write programs?
- maintain programs?
- use commercially available software?

Note: It would be interesting to record your answers to this question now, and compare them with the answers you would give after completing your studies in software engineering.

Exercise:

Make a collection of advertisements from the computer press. Categorise the jobs according to the skills required. How do software engineers compare with programmers and systems analysts in:

- the availability of work?
- the level of salary offered?

Chapter 2

Why engineer software?

2.1 Introduction

In this chapter, we develop some of the ideas introduced at the end of Chapter 1. We begin with the question, 'Why engineer software?' and consider the motives for developing software engineering techniques. We are able to identify 'quality software development' as the goal of our software engineering techniques, and we discuss just what we mean by this term.

2.2 The software crisis

In Chapter 1, we identified the situation which exists, where up to 80% of total software budgets is devoted to software maintenance. In other words, if the software had been designed to be free from errors and more flexible in the first place, it would be possible to save a massive amount of maintenance later.

This is one aspect of the software crisis. But the cost involved in software maintenance is not the only important issue; another is credibility. For a long time people have been suspicious of machines which take over work previously done by people, and the use of computers to undertake data-processing tasks has been unpopular. The fact that there has been significant publicity of some of the errors caused by the use of faulty computer programs in calculating gas bills and bank accounts has done nothing to help the image of the machine, which would, in any case, have been viewed with suspicion.

The additional fact that computers are used to monitor performance of safety-critical processes, such as chemical plants, oil refineries, military establishments and hospital intensive care units, makes it essential that the general public can be confident of the reliability of the machines undertaking the work.

Alongside this need for greater confidence in the quality and reliability of computers and software, we have seen a corresponding increase in the demand for software and in the availability of low-cost computers on which the software can be run.

There have therefore been two pressures on the software production industry which have done little to encourage an improvement in software quality:

- People with cheap computers have demanded software, which must be produced as cheaply as possible. Nobody is going to pay several times as much for each software package bought than the original cost of the computer (even though this might often be appropriate if the relative development and support costs are taken into account).
- There have been more and more people with access to computers which allow them to write software. These people are subject to no quality controls, and may release onto the market unreliable programs which have been badly designed and poorly written. These programs then take their places alongside the programs from responsible software producers and damage the reputation of the industry.

So we may summarise the main aspects of the software crisis like this:

1. There is massive demand for software.
2. There is a ready supply of low-quality software from unknown vendors at low cost.
3. Even some of the software produced by reputable companies has been known to be of dubious quality and doubtful flexibility.
4. The general public has little confidence in the quality of the software and the computers which operate it.

Against this background we need to discuss software engineering techniques. The term *software engineering* is intended to give a greater credibility to the design and build quality of the software which is produced. The theory is that engineers of other disciplines have a good reputation for the supply of high-quality products and therefore that software developed by software engineers will be of equally high quality and good design!

This attitude towards software developed by methods other than software engineering leads to an unjustified assumption that it was all bad. In fact, as we shall see in the pages which follow, some of the best approaches to software development from the days before the introduction of software engineering techniques have little to gain from a change to software engineering. In many respects, the change from conventional program development to a software engineering approach is more important in the way it makes a statement about what it is we are aiming for in our software development than it is in specifying the precise methods which we are going to use.

We shall see, therefore, that many of the techniques used in our software engineering developments mirror very closely those previously used in the system life cycle (see Chapter 3).

2.3   Quality software development

'Quality software development' is a very good way of describing the aim of software engineering, as it encapsulates the two principal aims of the software process:

1. We desire to produce high-quality software.
2. We aim to develop a method of designing and writing programs where the method itself is of high quality.

In other words, we are aiming to improve the quality, not just of the software which we produce, but of the software development process which we use for its production.

2.4   Quality development

There is nothing unique in looking for this twofold quality requirement. If you visit a builders merchant to buy bricks, you may well be offered some described as *Quality Assured to BS 5750*. It is reasonable to assume when we buy a pack of these bricks that British Standard 5750 describes what constitutes a well-made brick.

However, if we read higher education prospectuses, we may be surprised to discover that a certain B.Sc. course is also advertised as *Quality Assured to BS 5750*. This gives us some cause to reflect as to how both a packet of bricks and a B.Sc. course could be checked to satisfy the same British Standard!

Some packets of computer software also claim to be *Quality Assured to BS 5750*. This is because BS 5750 is all about the methods that an organisation adopts to control the quality of the output it produces. Thus a brick manufacturer might gain BS 5750 by describing how checks are made on the output to confirm its quality. And a university could describe how its courses and student performance are monitored to check up on the quality of the output. We might reflect for a moment as to whether, since dropping bricks from a great height is a good way to test their quality, perhaps doing the same with students would provide an equally good test of quality! Thus, in the same way, a software producer looking for a quality-controlled stamp of approval to BS 5750 would need to describe its procedures for monitoring that the software was being produced accurately.

Paradoxically, good quality control ensures that the producer knows the quality of the output, but it seems to give no guarantee to the user that the producer is only supplying production of high quality.

So *quality software development* certainly implies a rigorous quality control procedure built into the process. But what other features would a software producer look for?

- Speed of development. The software development process is notoriously slow. The production of a new item of software can typically be measured in person-years of work. Necessarily this is an expensive business, and any new approaches and additional tools or techniques which can speed up the process will be attractive even if they are offered at relatively high cost.
- Delivery to deadlines. The whole computer industry seems to be affected by companies which fail to live up to predicted target dates for the release of new products. Both hardware and software releases often happen well after the date originally advertised. This is partly because companies are always eager to advertise new products which offer an attractive alternative to those offered by their competitors, so that potential customers will know about the new items. However, at least equally relevant here is the fact that most software developments take far longer to complete than originally predicted. This can be caused by a number of problems:

  - Poor project management. Sometimes a project is inadequately planned and managed, so that time is wasted during the development process by people having to wait for critical stages in the process to be completed before work can commence on the next stage. Various management strategies are possible to assist in the management of a project and these can keep delays to a minimum. Some of these approaches are supported by project management software tools, which we shall discuss in Chapter 5.

  - Poor design or engineering. Probably the biggest single cause of delays in completion of software projects is the need to correct errors in the design or implementation of the programs themselves. Far too often, problems in the design do not appear until a very late stage in the development process, then they necessitate significant rewriting and redesigning of the programs. In addition, too much time is often required in testing the programs, because they have not been written to follow the design faithfully. Strategies which improve upon the fundamental quality control of the software under production are also likely to improve the timing of the output.

  - Rapid turnover of staff. The computing industry has, for a long time, suffered from a faster turnover of staff than most other industries. This is partly because of the rapid growth in the industry, which has not always been matched by a corresponding growth in the supply of well-qualified and experienced computer scientists, software engineers or analysts or whatever. Also, the problem is influenced by the fact that computing tends to attract a younger workforce who are in any case more mobile in their employment. All of this combines to make it more likely for a project to have to cope with several changes in personnel during its development period. If we add to this the fact that, even among well-qualified and responsible software development staff, there are wide-ranging differences in experience, approach and methods, all this can lead to further delays.

- Poor documentation. Closely linked to the previous item is the problem of poor documentation produced by staff during the software development process. For many software developers, solving problems and writing programs forms the interesting part of the work, and writing up the results in a suitable form of document is much less attractive. Therefore the documentation, which as we shall see, forms the basis of future modifications of the software, and also assists a new developer in the event of a change of staff, is often the least satisfactory part of the programmer's work. Of course, better management of the project could ensure that programmers and others involved in the software development process produced the required documentation and at the right time.

So there we have a description of the issues to be considered in assessing the quality of the software development process. We turn now to the question of the quality of the software.

2.5   What is quality software?

If you ask a software engineer or programmer what is meant by the term *high-quality software*, the answer you will receive will probably list some or all of the following:

- Software which works. So much software contains bugs, that it is certainly worth considering the question of whether a particular item of software is bug-free, or whether it still contains bugs which will cause it to produce the wrong answer, crash or perform in some other inappropriate way.
- Software which performs to its specification. Even some software apparently bug-free fails to perform to its specification. Whether the problem is that the program runs too slowly, or whether it is not quite as flexible to future changes as it should have been, software developers identify *performance to specification* as a key quality of software.
- Software which is well engineered and maintainable. Software which has been well written should be relatively easy to amend if the situation should arise. Therefore a software engineer who judged a program would often be looking to see how easy it would be to change the program if it needed to be changed.

On the other hand, perhaps the software engineers should not be given the job of determining what would constitute high-quality software. If you were a software user and were asked what would constitute *high-quality software* then what sort of answers would you give?

It is likely that you would start to think about what the software is like to use, rather than about whether the software works. This is because, as a consumer, we are used to having products that work and, considering questions of quality, we are looking beyond the simple matter of whether or not the product does the job we expected.

To consider an example from another field of engineering, imagine you buy a new car. What would you be looking for? Opinions vary as to what is actually required from a car, but you might consider:

- What the car looks like.
- How big the car is (e.g. will it take the family plus luggage for a holiday).
- Will the car fit in the garage?
- Does the car use a lot of fuel?
- Is the car easy to drive?
- What is the safety record of this model?
- Is the car reliable?

We would expect (and receive) some very odd responses if we began our visit to the car showroom by asking the car dealer whether the car works properly. This is important, but we just assume that it works without even asking.

In the same sort of way, we should be able to expect **any** piece of software purchased to **work** and it should only then be a case of considering *real* quality issues.

If you think about software applications which you use regularly, how do you distinguish between those which you like, and those which you do not? Probably your opinion is based upon one or more of the following:

- How easy is the software to use? Some software is easy to learn and use. Other software is not nearly so easy to use, for example it may use commands which are not logical nor easy to remember. Well-designed and high-quality software should address this problem of making the programs easy and natural to use in three possible ways:

    1. Some users find it attractive to have software which has a menu of options always visible to show what can be done.

    2. Some users find mouse-driven programs attractive and easy to use.

    3. Some users like programs which use a relatively small number of keystrokes to accomplish their chosen tasks, but the selection of *appropriate* keystrokes needs to be done carefully to help memorise them.

Thus the *user interface* provided by the software is of the utmost importance in judging software quality, and yet it is one of the issues often neglected by the programmer.

- How much error checking does the software undertake? The best software packages check inputs by the user for validity (i.e. whether the answer given is the correct *sort* of answer for the question being asked) and allow the user to verify the answers before processing takes place. This is based upon the assumption that mistakes are easier to rectify immediately than after processing has been done (and has to be undone). On the other hand, many users complain about those software packages which insist on asking *are you sure (y/n)* after each question is answered. The key to quality here is to aim for an appropriate balance between making it easy to correct mistakes, but also making it easy to enter the data without tiresome repetition.

- How quickly does the program execute? Whether this is an important issue depends largely upon what the actual program is used for:

  - If a program is in use in an interactive environment, that is one where a user and a computer conduct a conversation, then it is of the utmost importance that the user is not kept waiting for excessive periods, wasting expensive staff time.

  - If the program is run in batch mode, like many large computer applications traditionally undertaken without any continuous staff oversight, then it is less important that the programs run quickly.

- How large is the program? When computers were first used for applications, the cost of computers in general, and of their memory in particular, was so high that all programs sought to optimise the use of the available resources so that they would run in the most economical hardware. More recently, falling costs of hardware have meant that the size of the programs has become a secondary consideration compared to the desire for them to be user-friendly and to provide thorough error checking. However, most recently, the size of programs has begun to become an issue again, as more and more sophisticated applications are pushing the hardware to its limits. If a program can only operate on the most expensive sorts of computer system, then obviously its potential market is restricted to those who can afford this hardware platform. Nevertheless, size is probably seen as one of the least important quality issues.

- How flexible is the program? One fact about any software project is that it is an attempt to hit a moving target. The requirements identified today will have changed by the time the software is in use, and will probably change several more times during the supposed life of the software. It is therefore important that software should be sufficiently flexible to be adapted to meet these changing needs. How easy, hard or impossible it is for the software to be adapted in this way is dependent upon how well the software was designed with this aim in mind:

  1. Are add-ons available? In some cases, a software package is designed to meet a variety of specifications by plugging together appropriate modules from a range of compatible procedures. This means that software

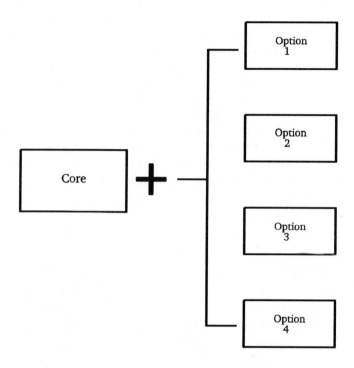

Figure 2.1 Selecting the appropriate options module gives a special-purpose software package

can be very flexible by offering the opportunity to buy extra modules when necessary (see Figure 2.1).

2. Can changes be made by the user? Where the purchase of add-ons is not possible, it is best if the user is able to make minor changes. Sometimes, software is designed with this in mind and is made *configurable,* so that the user can follow some instructions to make simple changes. More often, however, it is necessary to ask for parts of the software to be rewritten.

3. Can low-cost changes be made by the programmer? High-quality software can be designed in such a way as to be modular. This means that changes needed in the future should be confined to those modules which need to be changed to cope with new specifications. High-quality software should therefore be maintainable in this way at minimum expense. However, it is worth noting that if the software had been more thoughtfully specified in the first place, it could have been possible to have predicted the sorts of changes likely to be necessary and to have had the flexibility built-in to the system from the start!

- How good are the instructions provided? Whatever the software package and the experience of the user, it will always be necessary to examine the instructions provided with software at various stages. Instruction books can be of low quality, either because they are written by programmers (who are not particularly interested in writing instructions, and understand the system too well to write clearly about it anyway) or by technical documentors who have not fully understood the system. Choosing the right person to write the documentation is not easy, but more programs seem to be provided with good documentation today.

2.6 How do we measure software quality?

In this chapter we have explored the ideas which underlie software quality issues. Later in the book, we shall discuss how software quality can be *measured*, so that more accurate comparisons may be made between the quality of different programs.

2.7 Exercises

Self-test question

Why might simplicity of software be a feature for some users and a limitation for others?

Exercises

1. Choose a piece of software and write a report which analyses its quality.
2. Try to find out the average life span for some actual software packages in use in business.

Assignment

Interview three users of software packages and find out what they would look for in *high-quality software*. What would be necessary to convince them to change to a new system?

Chapter 3

Background to a project

3.1 Introduction

In this chapter we reflect upon the work which must be completed before the software engineering begins. We shall consider briefly the work of the systems analyst and set into context the roles of analyst and software engineer. The history of software development methods then sets the scene for discussions in subsequent chapters.

3.2 What the software engineer requires

If you were a software engineer beginning a project, then what information would you expect to be given? Our discussions in Chapter 1 identified the requirements definition as the starting point of the software engineer's work, so it is appropriate to consider, by way of background, the work which must be completed before a requirements definition can be drawn up.

The **requirements definition** document contains the following information:

1. A description of the organisation or company for which the software is to be developed.
2. An overview of the system and the way that different parts of it will inter-relate (known as the *system model*, see Chapter 5).
3. Details of the things which the system has to be able to do.
4. Details of the *qualities* which the system should exhibit. These are the sorts of things which we discussed in Chapter 2 and which form the basis of users' assessments of the quality of the software produced.
5. A description of any constraints on the system to be developed, such as those imposed by the desire to use existing hardware.

6. Details about the requirements to produce a flexible system which can be adapted to meet changing circumstances. So, for example, there should be a description here of the sorts of changes which might be envisaged in advance. We sometimes refer to this sort of description as the *maintenance information* for the system under development.

Later in this book, we shall give a thorough and more formal description of the requirements definition document. For the present, the purpose of identifying its broad content is to indicate the level of research and development work which must be undertaken before the work of the software engineer commences.

3.3   Developing a new system

The impetus to develop a new system must come from a recognition by the management of an organisation of some inadequacy in the existing practices. This recognition of a problem is sometimes termed the 'Trigger' for the development of a new system. Management might identify a need, but they are rarely expert at identifying whether an appropriate strategy for fulfilling the need can come from the development of a new computer system. It is therefore normal to call upon experts in the analysis of requirements to come into the organisation and produce a report on the feasibility of solving the problems.

This *feasibility study* undertaken by *systems analysts* seeks to answer the following questions:

1. Does the problem actually exist as it is perceived by the management? Should a different problem be tackled?
2. Is it likely to be possible to provide a solution to the problem which is:

   - economical, in terms of the likely costs and benefits derived

   - an improvement on existing experience

   - deliverable in a reasonable time?

The systems analysts will undertake an initial investigation. After the investigation they will produce a report which indicates:

1. What the problem to be solved is.
2. Whether it is likely to be soluble.
3. How long it will take to solve.
4. What the likely costs of solution are.
5. What the likely benefits of the project are.
6. A recommendation as to whether the work should be undertaken.

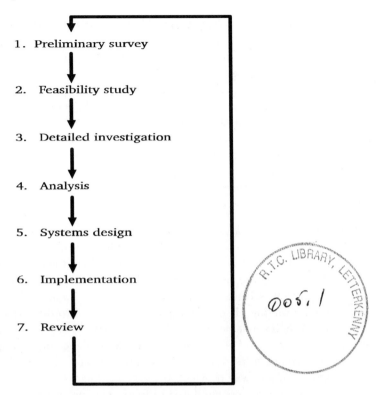

1. Preliminary survey

2. Feasibility study

3. Detailed investigation

4. Analysis

5. Systems design

6. Implementation

7. Review

Figure 3.1 The systems life cycle

This feasibility study constitutes the first stage in a conventional *systems life-cycle* approach to software development. The stages in a traditional systems life cycle are shown in Figure 3.1. The systems life cycle is made up of a series of stages, which begin with the feasibility study and end with the review and maintenance of the software implemented. In between come the more detailed analysis of the requirements of the new system, the design of the system and its implementation and testing. Finally it is put into operation in place of the previous system. The review and maintenance phase of the life cycle represents a regular reconsideration of the package as implemented against current requirements. As indicated earlier, requirements change over time, and therefore a system which is exactly right when it is first written will become gradually less appropriate. Decisions to amend the existing system or to replace it with a new one form a built-in trigger to the next turn of the systems life cycle.

We first introduced the idea of a life cycle in Chapter 1 (Figure 1.1), where we identified the key stages in a software development project. It is interesting to compare the traditional systems life-cycle model for systems analysis (Figure 3.1) with the software engineering life cycle.

3.4   What is wrong with the systems life cycle?

Software development followed the systems life-cycle model for many years, and still does in many organisations. And the systems life-cycle approach has been responsible for the development of much software of high quality. It has also been the natural development method during the *software crisis* and as a result it has lost some credibility. Nevertheless, the methods which were employed in the systems life cycle formed the basis for almost all the more up-to-date methods of developing software. Newer methods simply take older ideas and add rigorous methodologies to remove the scope for error.

We may identify three particular weaknesses of the system life-cycle approach to program development:

1. The systems analyst is in control of the entire life cycle. The software development process contains two distinct phases: first, the problem is to establish requirements. Interviews with staff often form the basis of this investigation. This means the interpersonal skills of the systems analyst are particularly important; second, the skills required centre upon analysis, design and technical thinking. It can be argued that these two distinct qualities are rarely found in a single person. It is certainly true that any person who undertakes all the stages of the systems life cycle must be less of a specialist than one who concentrates on either the interpersonal or the technical skills alone. One common way in which the systems life-cycle approach is operated is to have programmers employed to follow the instructions of a systems analyst. This has the advantage of ensuring that those who write the programs are specialists in the area, but also has the effect of making the programming task a less highly regarded stage in the process than the analysis and design. This in turn may have unfortunate consequences for the quality of the programs written.

2. There is a lack of confidence in software produced in conventional ways. Whether the conventional ways are good or bad is largely irrelevant here. The fact is that the development of reliable computer software is believed by many people to be impossible. Therefore the very fact that the systems life-cycle approach is put to one side in favour of a new method can bring benefits in the attitude of staff towards the software developed.

3. The systems life-cycle approach does not dictate any particular methodology, nor any particular rigour. Therefore, as in any uncontrolled industry, there can be those who undertake the work thoroughly and those who do not. The approach makes no particular demands as to quality or standards and therefore it is very difficult to discriminate in any meaningful way between the best practices and those which are less good.

3.5 So what is special about software engineering?

Software engineering is a very difficult term to define. We tried to give a definition in Chapter 1, and found that the only satisfactory thing to do was to identify various stages in the software development process, and to define the work of the software engineer as being concerned with proceeding through these stages in a particular project. However, having identified the stages in a conventional systems life cycle, and noted the limitations found in this approach, we are in a position to make some fairly clear-cut definitions of the methods and characteristics, which we will describe as software engineering:

- The adoption of a particular set of methods, clearly defined and rigorously applied to the software development process.
- The subdivision of the early stages of problem definition from the later stages of program design and implementation. For convenience, we shall describe the people who undertake the early investigations as **systems analysts**, and those who work on the programs as **software engineers**, although we recognise that there is not really any clear-cut distinction between these two groups.
- The desire to have *high-quality software development* as the main goal of the process.

3.6 Adopting rigorous standards and methods

As we have identified in Section 3.5, the adoption of suitable rigorous methods and standards is crucial to the whole software engineering process. There are many alternative methodologies proposed by different authors, and in any book on software engineering it is necessary to select a particular one for the examples and discussions. Most of the methods provide a broadly comparable structure, involving the use of diagrams and text for descriptions of the system to be implemented, and the imposition of standards to help to control the quality of the development process at various stages.

We have chosen to describe methods based upon structured systems analysis and design methodology (SSADM) which is a method adopted by the UK Government for all software development in Government and related organisations. However, although the actual form of diagrams which we will show are specifically appropriate to SSADM, most of the discussion which we give is equally appropriate to other methods.

3.7   Choosing a method

Much software development is haphazard and lacks method. For this reason, it can be argued that the precise method selected is of secondary importance, and that the most important thing is that some method or other should be chosen. This is an over-simplification, but it is nevertheless true that choosing a method simply to suit a particular application is usually inappropriate. The choice of method is more of a long-term strategic decision for an organisation to take.

Most organisations which have adopted software engineering methods and ideals have selected a methodology which is used throughout the organisation. Unless there is very good reason, it will not be possible for a particular software developer to choose to use an alternative. Nor would it be wise, because various tools which help in the software development process are available, and almost all are tied to a particular method. Therefore the choice of a method other than the one favoured by the organisation would almost certainly make the project harder to complete on time, and less well integrated into the organisation's documentation and system requirements.

3.8   Exercises

Self-Test Question

What might constitute the trigger for:

(a) computerising supermarket checkouts?
(b) installing a new payroll system?

Exercise

Look again at the job advertisements in the computer press. Establish the distribution of current vacancies between programmers, analysts and software engineers. Do the adverts distinguish the roles in the same ways that we have?

Assignment

How does the job description of a software engineer differ from that of an analyst programmer? (You may find it useful to contact one or two employers to gain an up-to-date answer to this question.)

Chapter 4

Issues, methodologies and techniques

4.1 Introduction

This chapter focuses on some of the issues involved in developing computer systems. We look at why different systems development methodologies are currently available, and consider in detail the methodology known as SSADM. The relationship between SSADM and software engineering is the key to understanding later chapters and we introduce some of the important techniques used in the system development process.

4.2 An overview of the issues

In Chapter 3 we discussed some of the shortcomings of the *systems life-cycle model*. A number of issues are important in this area. These issues are discussed in the following sections.

4.2.1 Reductionism versus general systems theory

A reductionist approach uses techniques which centre upon splitting the system being considered into its component parts. Sometimes it might be more appropriate to look at the system as a whole and identify characteristics of the whole system. General systems theory is based upon the belief that systems can only be understood when viewed as a whole. This tends to be particularly suitable for *soft*, ill-defined problems. These problems usually arise in systems where people play a central role.

Two particular methodologies are important in applying general systems theory. They are effective technical and human implementation of computer-based systems (ETHICS) (see Appendix III) and soft systems methodology (SSM). SSM was developed at the University of Lancaster by Checkland (see Checkland 1990). It concentrates on the *analysis* stage of system development. This is common amongst soft methodologies. The heart of SSM is a diagram known as the **Rich Picture**. The Rich Picture is very different from the diagrams we will be looking at in Section 4.7, as it does not break the system down into the different processes that occur and the data necessary for these processes. Instead, it identifies the *groups of people* involved, the *relevant issues*, the *system boundaries*, the *external influences* and so on. The Rich Picture would be developed by a team of people involved in a hospital operation, assisted by the analyst. Thus the team might include patients, medical staff, administrative staff and management.

General systems theory has been a growth area for the last 20 years and has developed in an interdisciplinary fashion, the ideas originating from such diverse areas as sociology, biology and political science.

In contrast, reductionism is based upon scientific methods which have been pivotal in scientific research for hundreds of years. It is based on the assumption that the world is complex and that we need to simplify it in order to increase our understanding. Thus a valid approach might be to pick out one aspect of the world and try to understand that in the hope of being able to generalise our findings. A second aspect of reductionism is the process of breaking problems down into subproblems. It is believed that this repeated subdivision should eventually result in problems which are sufficiently simple to solve.

For example, a programmer asked to produce a program to control the company payroll, might start by considering the part of the problem concerned with producing pay slips and then the part concerned with management statistics. Clearly, the two tasks are not independent, as there will be one or more common databases. This emphasises one of the problems with reductionism: identifying *independent* subproblems can be difficult. Reductionism, as a technique in system development, is usually used in methodologies such as SSADM, STRADIS (Gane and Sarson 1979) and JSD (Jackson 1983). These are known as *hard* methodologies and are typically used in situations where the problem is well defined. The example given above of implementing a payroll is well defined. In contrast, a task to identify why a school is failing to attract pupils would be a poorly defined task. The techniques such hard methodologies specify usually involve identifying the major operations which occur within the system and the data necessary to perform these operations.

It is in the nature of sofware engineering that hard methodologies will be most prominent throughout this book.

4.2.2   Closed versus open systems

Many approaches require the system developer to analyse and design a system based upon a very clear *specification*. For example an analyst/programmer might be asked to develop a personnel database. This is known as a closed system approach and has the disadvantage that the analyst/programmer is not given the opportunity to analyse any external factors. For example, in an organisation where difficulties are being experienced in keeping the personnel information up to date, the solution might be thought to be establishing a personnel database, whereas in reality a more appropriate solution might be to move the personnel office nearer to the workforce, enabling more frequent interaction. An approach which allows the external factors to be considered is known as an *open systems* approach.

Hard system methodologies tend to make the assumption that the system being developed or altered is closed. In other words there is no need to consider external factors which might impact upon the system. In the case of a payroll system this is fairly reasonable. Nevertheless there is still the possibility that an external factor such as tax rules might change, rendering the system incorrect. So it would be sensible to check any legislation currently going through Parliament. The consideration of such open system issues clearly impacts upon the *maintenance* stage of the systems life cycle. It is suprising how few systems are completely closed.

The software engineering approach usually starts with the requirements definition, which should be developed taking into account any relevant open system issues. Other system development methodologies vary in how they tackle these issues. For example, information engineering (IE) focuses system development upon the business plan of the organisation concerned. Such a business plan would need to take into account the current and anticipated business context. Thus the economic climate, the influence of rival companies and so on would be considered. This type of approach is less obviously appropriate to a hospital or school, so different techniques can be employed. ETHICS, which we consider in Appendix II, can be more suited to this type of situation.

4.2.3   Socio-technical systems approach

This approach started to be developed in the 1960s. It is based around two beliefs:

1. All systems are open.
2. The system's environment, the group dynamics of the individuals within the system and the technology involved are all interdependent.

Thus if a school were to implement a computerised system for individual pupil profiles, it would be necessary to consider the following issues:

1. Environmental factors: The school governors, the local community, other schools, the local education authority, etc.
2. The group dynamics: Who would have access to the system? Where would the system be sited? If it is sited in the secretary's office, would this give him or her a disproportionate amount of power?
3. The technology: What is the most appropriate computer hardware and software?

These areas are interdependent, so additional issues might arise:

- What technology is used by other schools?
- What will be the attitude of the local community to the school's increased efficiency?

The socio-technical approach has developed independently of the systems movement, but the two approaches have much in common. ETHICS is a good example of a system development methodology based around the socio-technical approach.

4.2.4   Analyst versus user-centred system development

In the traditional systems life cycle, the analyst went into the organisation and observed. This observation might have involved the use of questionnaires, interviews, time and motion studies and so on. This led to the analysis, design and implementation. The approach is essentially analyst centred which means that those most *involved* in using the system are peripheral to the system development process. This has a number of dangers:

- The analyst may not fully understand the workings of the system, being unaware of tensions between individuals, short cuts which are sometimes taken, and so on.
- The analyst's presence may produce resentment in the workforce. No-one likes a complete stranger coming into their place of work and telling them what they are doing wrong. This may result in a lack of cooperation.
- The final system may not meet the acceptability criteria of the users. The users will have opinions about what the system should do and how it should do it. If these are not met, the system may well be underutilised. For example, if a secretary was given a computer-based diary, it might well be seen as an irrelevance to the job and not be used.

One way to overcome this is to increase the amount of user participation. This has the added advantage of providing greater access to the real experts in the problem area: the people who operate the system. There are different levels of user participation identified by Mumford (1983a). The one just described is usually referred to as *consultative participation*. The second level is know as *representative participation* and allows for a design group which includes both analysts and systems users. All members of the design group would be of equal importance. Thus the analysts could, in principle, be overruled by the users. It would be important for the user representatives to be chosen from all levels within the organisation. One advantage of this approach is that a number of different user perspectives will be represented. These perspectives can be startlingly different. For example, in a hospital, the views of the patients, doctors and the management are likely to be radically different:

- The doctors will be concerned with the well-being of a large number of patients in wards around the whole hospital, but their knowledge of the working of any one ward will be limited.
- Each patient will be concerned with their own well-being and they will have a clear view of how well the ward is succeeding in meeting their needs.
- The management will only have a limited perspective on the medical side of the organisation, but they will be aware of the financial implications of any decisions made.

For the successful development of a system within a hospital it may well be necessary to consider all these perspectives. This may not be easy because there will be political and ideological tensions. However if people are given the opportunity to resolve these tensions during the system development, the final system is more likely to be accepted and used by all concerned.

The third level of participation is *consensus participation*. At this level, all users are involved in the analysis and design process. This could be seen as an ideal, but it can be difficult to implement and time consuming. One approach might be only to consult users about the part of the system which relates to them.

A related problem is the expertise required of the users involved in the participation process. Different methodologies use different techniques in the analysis and design stages. For example, software engineering may utilise *formal methods* (see Appendix I) for specifying the system requirements. This would be inappropriate for use in a system development methodology with a high level of participation. ISAC is a Swedish methodology in which the analysis and design stages are performed entirely by the system users guided by an analyst. In ISAC these stages are performed by the use of various diagramming techniques, developed to be used readily by any member of the workforce.

4.2.5 Informal prototyping

When students are learning to write computer programs, they usually start by adopting an informal prototyping methodology: they write some code, see if it works, alter it in order to improve it and so on. This cycle then continues until a working program is achieved. This is a reasonable strategy when you are trying to understand the function of the different commands; however, most experienced programmers find that this approach proves unsatisfactory when the problem is reasonably complex. This is because, every time the program is altered, there is a chance of introducing new errors. Also it is very easy to lose track of the program, forgetting why a particular piece of code was written and so on. For these reasons, the current trend is away from informal prototyping and towards specifying the program design in detail before touching the computer. This issue is at the heart of software engineering.

As we shall see, prototyping is still useful when handling issues which are poorly understood. For example, when developing a human-computer interface, it is common practice to develop a prototype interface, test it on potential users, then alter it accordingly. In this scenario, the users are only partially understood and it is difficult to predict with any certainty their reaction to the interface.

4.3   What is a methodology?

We have used the term *methodology* several times already, without defining it. For our purposes it will be best to think of a methodology as being made up of:

- a number of predefined steps
- each step may involve techniques such as data-flow diagrams (see below)
- each step may involve software tools such as computer aided software engineering (CASE) tools (see Chapter 5).

This can be summarised in the expression:

Methodology = Steps + Techniques + Tools

The systems life-cycle model is an example of a methodology. There are a number of steps which need to be carried out and these use a variety of techniques, such as interviewing and analysis according to the *principles of procedure*. There may also be software tools to support the whole process.

Methodologies usually also have an underlying philosophy. The philosophy which underlies the systems life cycle is that computerisation is usually the best solution and that the analyst/programmer is the best person to perform it. Different philosophies link in different ways with the issues described in Section 4.2. For example, a methodology may have the philosophy that user satisfaction is the key to the success of any system. This in turn will lead to the use of user-centred techniques, such as design groups made up of users from all levels within the organisation.

Identifying the philosophy can be a useful way of distinguishing between methodologies, as the descriptions of SSADM and ETHICS demonstrate. However the comparison of methodologies is fraught with difficulties, since most methodologies are constantly updated and different practitioners tend to implement the same methodology in slightly different ways. For more information see Avison and Fitzgerald (1988), Benyon and Skidmore (1987) and Jayaratna (1986).

4.4   Structured systems analysis and design methodology (SSADM)

SSADM is founded in computer science and is consequently based around semi-formal, reductionist techniques. In contrast to user-centred approaches, user participation and general organisational issues are treated as being of secondary importance. It is widely used in industry, particularly in the United Kingdom. There are numerous books on SSADM; particularly useful are the series of manuals produced by the National Computer Centre (NCC) (Longworth and Nicholls 1986 and Nicholls 1987).

There is no explicitly stated philosophy in SSADM. However, it is possible to infer the following:

- SSADM imposes a detailed and rigid structure on the system development.
- It is based upon the belief that a prescriptive approach to system development is possible.
- This is consistent with a low level of user participation.

The majority of techniques used by SSADM are reductionist. Thus system development is perceived to be the process of splitting the system into its component parts and considering each in turn. This approach tends to disregard holistic issues and considers the problem as a closed system.

According to Nicholls (1987), there are three other issues to be considered:

- SSADM forces the developer to look at the system from three viewpoints:

  1. the data used within the system
  2. the processes that operate upon the data
  3. the events which occur during the system operation.

  This approach increases the likelihood of all the potential problems being detected.
- SSADM is self-documenting. All the techniques employed are diagrammatic, so if the system developer keeps a file of these diagrams, along with a small amount of supporting text, by the time the system is complete it will also be fully documented.
- There is a distinction made between logical and physical representations. A logical representation specifies what the system should do and a physical representation indicates how it will do it. This is important because it allows the system developer to separate the issues.

There are six phases in SSADM. Each of these is subdivided into a number of steps. The steps are partially ordered. In other words, all the steps need to be carried out, but some of them have to be performed before others. At the end of the first two stages there is a *quality assurance review,* involving the system developers and the users, which ensures that the project is proceeding to plan. The stages are as follows.

4.4.1   Analysis phase

- **Stage 1: Investigation of current system.** As the name suggests, this involves studying the existing system and identifying any problems. One of the most important outcomes of this stage is the problems and requirements list, which influences the subsequent stages in the system development. The major techniques used in this stage are data-flow diagrams and entity-relationship diagrams (entity models and entity life histories) which are described later in this chapter. The emphasis is on modelling the physical system, representing what is actually happening.

- **Stage 2: Specify required system.** The objective of this stage is to produce an agreed system model. This will include data-flow diagrams, entity-relationship diagrams and entity life histories all outlining the operation of the proposed system. It also takes into account the audit, system controls and security issues. A key factor in the development of this model is the involvement of the users in prioritising the problems and requirements list, and establishing which of these should be handled by the new system, based upon a crude cost-benefit analysis.

- **Stage 3:   Create Technical Options.** There are usually a number of ways of implementing the system model. For example, the system developer will need to consider which parts of the system are to be manual and which automated. For the automated parts, the type of computer, peripherals and so on will be considered. Having identified the options, these need to be evaluated, using such techniques as cost/benefit analysis and impact analysis. The users are then involved in the choice of the most appropriate option.

4.4.2   Design phase

- **Stage 4:   Data design.** This stage merges the bottom-up analysis of the data requirements as specified by the users with the required entity-relationship diagram passed through from stage 2. The bottom-up analysis involves organising the data into tables, which can then be put into *third normal form* (see below). The resulting tables can then be compared with the required entity-relationship diagram. This results in a composite logical design (CLD) which can be converted into a database design.

- **Stage 5: Process design.** The users have specified the system requirements in stage 2 and the CLD has been developed, so it is necessary to ensure that the CLD can meet these requirements. This might involve developing some type of prototype.

- **Stage 6:   Physical design.** The outcome of this stage is the program specifications and database/file definitions. Thus the logical designs need to be translated into a physical form.

It can be seen from this description that the system development process is very rigorous and prescriptive. The belief is that if the stages are followed through in detail, a successful system will be developed and the design issues are considered in particular detail. Very little consideration is given to the details of the implementation. Thus any actual programming would need to be carried out using separate techniques, such as those used in the software engineering cycle.

There are numerous software tools which support SSADM, in particular Excelerator and Systems Engineer. The role of this type of tool is outlined in Chapter 5. Diagrammatic techniques are used throughout SSADM. Some of these techniques are outlined later in this chapter.

4.5 The relationship between SSADM and software engineering

Software engineering has as its key stages:

- Software specification
  (Requirements definition, followed by requirements specification)
- Software design
- Software implementation
- Software maintenance.

All the stages in software engineering refer explicitly to software. In contrast, the two methodologies outlined are more concerned with systems, the software development occurring at quite a late stage. This suggests that the methodologies have a broader view of the development process. Secondly, the methodologies only deal with the software implementation and maintenance phases very briefly, whereas software engineering concentrates on these areas. In fact the desire to write *correct* programs is the origin of the field. Thus software engineering can be seen to complement many methodologies, including SSADM. SSADM is highly prescriptive: each stage is to be completed in detail before the next one. In contrast, software engineering, as it has developed over the years, is like a tool box, where the appropriate technique is selected for a particular situation.

The stages in SSADM relate to software engineering in the following ways:

- SSADM Stage 1: Investigation of current system. There is no parallel to this stage in software engineering, as the first stage is software specification and this assumes that some form of analysis of the problem/existing system has already occurred. The outcome of this stage: the problems and requirements list has similarities to the requirements definition (see Chapter 7).
- SSADM Stage 2: Specify required system. This stage is similar to deriving the requirements specification in software engineering. However, the techniques used tend to differ. In SSADM the various pictorial methods are

dominant, whilst in software engineering formal methods (as described in Appendix I) are dominant. A further distinction is that in SSADM, because the diagrams are used, there is some confusion between the specification and the design. In contrast, formal methods are used to produce a specification of what the system should do and this specification is quite separate from any design issues.

- SSADM Stage 3: Create technical options. SSADM takes a broader view of the development process and consequently consider other issues in addition to the software issues. Thus there is no overlap between SSADM and software engineering at this stage.

- SSADM Stages 4-6: Data design, process design and physical design. In SSADM, these stages deal with manual and automated parts of the system. Apart from this difference, these stages correspond to system design in software engineering. The manner in which this phase is implemented does, however, differ. Software engineering presents a range of possible approaches, such as structured design, object-oriented design and real-time design. In contrast, SSADM is highly prescriptive giving rigid guidelines for developing the design.

The software implementation and maintenance stages in software engineering have no parallel in SSADM.

In the remainder of this book, we focus some of the discussion of software engineering around concepts which originate in SSADM. This occurs mainly in Chapters 6 and 8. In Chapter 6 the discussion of systems analysis will focus on SSADM, as this is not covered by the software engineering life cycle. In Chapter 8, which covers system design, the description will be based around SSADM, both to provide continuity and to show how the ideas can be utilised in the software engineering life cycle. In neither chapter will SSADM be adhered to rigidly; instead the ideas and principles will be emphasised and practical examples given.

4.6   Supporting techniques

Structured techniques originated in the early days of software engineering and originally focused upon the implementation phase. Since then it has been realised that the same techniques can be applied to the design, analysis and fact-finding stages. This means that structured techniques can now be introduced in the fact-finding phase, evaluated in the analysis phase, modified in the design phase and used for guidance in the implementation. This provides a new continuity to the system development and forms the basis of SSADM and other similar design methodologies.

Structured techniques can be grouped according to four perspectives on the system:

1. The process view

2. The data view
3. The time view
4. The decision view.

Some of the techniques are not used in SSADM. This is because the software engineering cycle is broader and less prescriptive than that of SSADM.

The techniques which SSADM uses in the analysis and design stages of the systems life cycle are mostly diagramatic and can be grouped according to three views of the system:

- Process view. Every system contains a number of operations which need to occur in order for the system to operate. These operations are referred to as processes and are represented in context diagrams and data-flow diagrams.
- Data view. Most systems contain a significant amount of stored data. For example, a shop may have customer lists, stock lists and so on. This data is represented in both third normal form, which is a tabular representation and in entity models. Both approaches are useful, because the former is bottom-up and the latter is top-down, so the two can be merged to ensure the correct design.
- Event view. Events alter the data in a system. The sale of an item in a shop is an event because it causes the stock data to be altered. Events are represented in entity-life histories.

There are other relevant techniques but for brevity these will be omitted. Different methodologies may have different symbols for the same concepts. For more detail on the various available techniques, see Cutts (1991). In this chapter each technique will be described very briefly using an example. They will be covered in more detail in Chapters 6 and 8, where they will be applied to a more complex example. Throughout this section, the examples will be based on the system underlying a dentist's surgery.

4.6.1 Process view

When we approach an existing system, it is often simplest to start the analysis by identifying the various processes which occur within the system and the data which need to be passed between them. They can then be checked for completeness and correctness. This analysis then forms the basis of the design for the new system (most new systems adopt many aspects of the existing system; why throw out the baby with the bath water?).

The representation of the processes and data-flow is initiated by the usual fact-finding techniques of observation, questionnaires and interviews. The development of this representation is not an easy task and is usually achieved in a top-down manner, starting with a context diagram. As the name suggests, the context

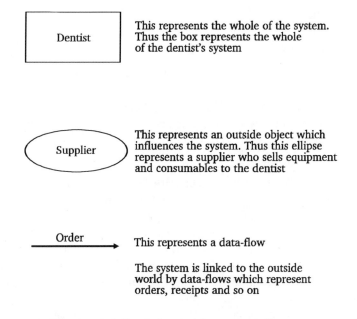

Figure 4.1 Symbols used in context diagrams

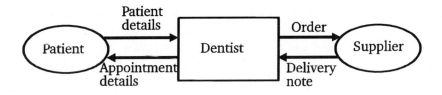

Figure 4.2 A context diagram

diagram places the system in its envionment, identifying all the outside influences and the data-flows between the system and its environment.

The context diagram is translated into a data-flow diagram, which can be expanded repeatedly until the required level of detail is achieved. This results in a hierarchy of data-flow diagrams, with the least detailed being at level 0, the expansion of level 0 being level 1 and so on. Figure 4.1 illustrates the range of symbols used in a context diagram and Figure 4.2 represents the following information:

There are two objects outside of the system, but relevant to it: the patients and the suppliers. The patients provide their details in order to register and they receive appointment details and so on. The dentist orders stock from the supplier, who then provides the stock, along with a delivery note. Apart from these external issues, the system is treated as being closed.

Figure 4.3 illustrates the symbols used in data-flow diagrams and Figure 4.4

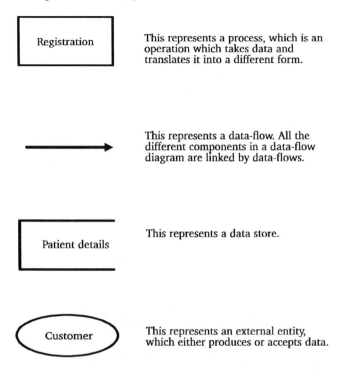

This represents a process, which is an operation which takes data and translates it into a different form.

This represents a data-flow. All the different components in a data-flow diagram are linked by data-flows.

This represents a data store.

This represents an external entity, which either produces or accepts data.

Figure 4.3 Symbols used in data-flow diagrams

represents a small part of a data-flow diagram for the scenario described above.

4.6.2 Data view

In many systems, the data stored is considered to be more stable than the processes that operate upon it. Thus an important view of the system is that of the data which need to be stored and manipulated. As we have seen, data-flow diagrams have data stores, but these are a relatively crude representation and more detail is necessary.

A key concept in this area is the entity. An entity is an area about which information needs to be stored. Thus in the dentist example, *Patient* would be an entity. At the analysis stage the identification of the entities and the relationships between them is critical. These can then be represented by an entity model. During the development process, the model can be checked for completeness and correctness. As with the process view, it will probably form the basis of the design for the new system. The entity model is usually augmented by a list of the attributes associated with each entity. Attributes are equivalent to fields in a record.

The data can also be analysed by evaluating all the documents (and computer

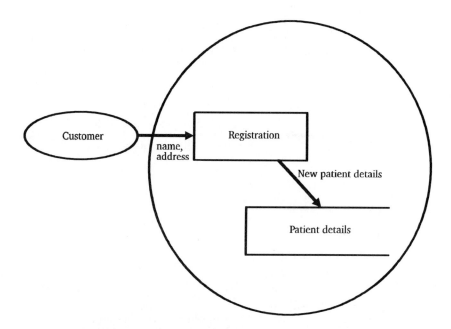

Figure 4.4 A data-flow diagram

records, if appropriate) which are currently used for storing data. These documents are then converted into tabular form which can be simplified using a process known as normalisation; a mathematical technique developed by Codd (1970). Each of these tables then corresponds to a single entity in the entity model.

Entity modelling is useful for understanding the current system. This understanding can then be made more detailed by cross-checking the model with the normalised tables. The approach then combines top-down analysis (entity modelling) with bottom-up analysis (normalisation). Entity models contain the symbols illustrated in Figure 4.5.

The normalised tables equivalent to the Patient and Appointment entities are illustrated in Figure 4.6. Each column represents an attribute and each row an instance of the entity. Thus the first patient is Fred Bloggs who lives at 10 Railway Cuttings and whose identifier is 99. It can be seen that he has made two appointments as two rows in the appointment table have an ID of 99. Thus each row in *patient* can correspond to several rows in *appointment*: this is the way in which one to many relationships are actually implemented. The derivation of normalised tables is explained in Chapter 8.

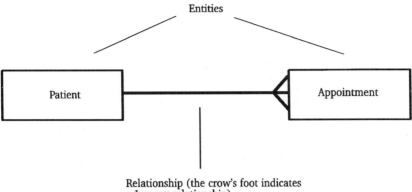

Figure 4.5 An entity model

Patient

ID	Name	Address
99	Fred Bloggs	10, Railway Cuttings
201	Mary Jones	25, The Street
555	Joe Hampton	80, London Road

Appointment

ID	Day	Time
99	Mon	16.30
90	Wed	14.00
99	Fri	10.00
201	Tues	14.30

Figure 4.6 Normalised tables

4.6.3 Event view

Once the process and data views have been considered, it is necessary to look at the event view. An event is an occurrence which results in data being altered: events may create, alter or delete data. Each event may be the consequence of a process or an external source updating a data store. In order to understand the implications of the event, it is not sufficient to look at the data-flow diagram, as each data store may represent several entities. Thus we have to cross-reference the data-flow diagram with the entities in the entity model. This analysis results in

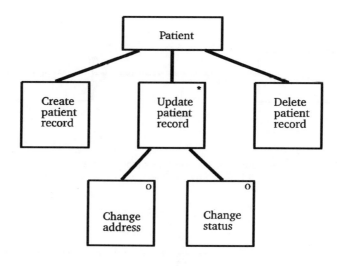

* Indicates that a procedure
is to be repeated.

o Indicates a choice

Figure 4.7 An entity life history

the development of an entity life history for each entity.

The reason for developing entity life histories is that the events which operate upon an entity often need to occur in a particular order. A fault would occur if this order is violated. For example, we should not be permitted to attempt to alter the address of a patient who is not currently registered.

In SSADM, entity life histories have similar syntax to Jackson structure diagrams. They contain the symbols illustrated in Figure 4.7. We can interpret Figure 4.7 as follows:

The first event that occurs is the creation of the patient record. This will be a consequence of the Registration process illustrated earlier. This will be followed by a number of updates. These can take the form of changes of address or change of status. The final event would be the deletion of the patient record, if the patient were to move on for some reason.

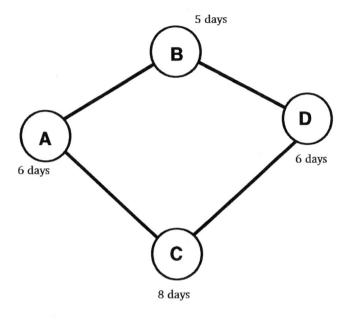

5 days

B

D

A

6 days

6 days

C

8 days

Figure 4.8 An activity network

4.7 Project planning techniques

A methodology alone is insufficient for the successful completion of a software development project. A high percentage of software projects run over time and over
budget, resulting in serious losses. The way to avoid this is through project planning, which enables the costs involved and the time which the project is likely
to take to be predicted. It is also concerned with monitoring the progress of the
project, resequencing the various activities where necessary and ensuring the highest level of quality possible. The major techniques used in project planning are
activity networks and bar charts.

Project management is a key to quality software development and we consider
it in more detail later. Here we draw attention to some relevant techniques.

Activity networks represent graphically the different activites which need to
occur during the project. It represents the duration of the activities and their
interdependencies. An example activity net is given in Figure 4.8. This indicates
that A must occur before activity B and C, and both B and C must occur before
D. B and C can occur in parallel. It also states the length of each activity.

Drawing up this network will be complex and time consuming. It is also subject
to change as unforeseen difficulties occur. However the identification of *parallel
activities* can reduce the project duration significantly and the network enables the
software house to predict when the new system should be complete.

A further important function of the network is to enable the project management

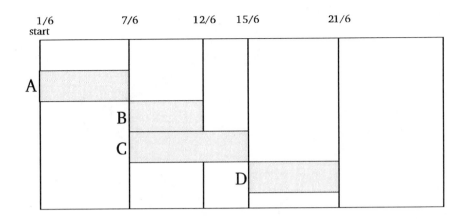

Figure 4.9 A bar chart

to identify the *critical* activites. Critical activities are activities which will cause the project duration to be extended if they overrun. In Figure 4.8, the minimum project duration is 20 days. This is reached by adding the durations of A, C and D. Thus each of these activities is critical and together they form the critical path. B has more flexibility, as it can take up to 8 days before it affects the total project duration. Separating the activities in this way is useful, as it allows the project managers to give the highest priority to the completion of the critical activites.

When drawing up a network, it is also important to take into account the re-sources necessary for each activity. For example, two activities might require the use of a single piece of software. In this case a decision needs to be made: either the activities are performed sequentially or a second copy of the software is bought so they can be performed in parallel. The first solution increases the project duration and the second requires expenditure on additional software. This sort of trade off is quite common. It is necessary to ensure that all the resources are used efficiently throughout the duration of the project.

The PERT chart is an augmented activity chart which also includes estimates of optimistic, pessimistic and likely durations for each activities. This makes the critical path analysis more complex and usually requires the use of some form of project management software tool (see Chapter 5).

An alternative representation is the bar chart or Gantt chart. This effectively represents the same information, but in a slightly different form. The bar chart in Figure 4.9, is equivalent to the activity chart in Figure 4.8, but it lists the actual dates for the start and completion of each activity. This will make the monitoring of the project's execution simpler, as it will be possible to see which activities should be happening at any given moment.

It is likely that the activity chart will be developed during the planning stage and it will then be translated into a bar chart to enable effective monitoring of the project's execution. However, both will be subject to change when problems arise.

The activity charts and bar charts will be augmented by tabular information concerning the resources required by each activity, staff allocations and so on.

4.8 Exercises

Self-test questions

1. Is a hard methodology easier or harder to use than a soft methodology in computer systems development?
2. How can project planning help in software development?

Exercises

1. Try to identify some aspects of the *philosophy* which underpins your software writing.
2. Which types of diagrams do you find the most useful in software development, and why?

Assignment

Determine the software development methodologies of some local organisations. Do they employ in-house software engineers or bring in specialist contractors?

Chapter 5

Software tools and their role in software engineering

5.1 Introduction

In this chapter we shall meet a variety of software tools which may be used to assist the software development process. We shall discuss in some detail the various types of CASE tools used in the industry, and we shall also consider the use of other types of software to assist the work of the software engineer. We shall pay particular attention to the methods discussed in Chapter 4 and the relationships between chosen methodologies and the software which helps in their application.

5.2 Computers in other branches of engineering

From the start of this book, we have been concerned with the problem of improving the software development process to increase the speed of production of new computer software, while at the same time improving the quality of the software produced. We will consider the questions of quality in more detail elsewhere, but we are particularly concerned in ensuring that software produced conforms to the specification it was designed to meet, and that the specification is as accurate and appropriate as possible to the needs of the client.

The introduction of *engineering* methods within the software development process was identified as being a particularly significant step, in that it offered the opportunity to take a new look at the current practices in software development, and consider how methods and ideas from other branches of engineering could be applied in software development. One such method, which became very widely adopted in other branches of engineering over the 1980s, is the use of computer aided design (CAD) tools.

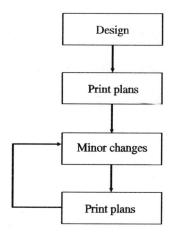

Figure 5.1   The CAD package allows plans to be reprinted to take account of changes without redrawing the entire plan

5.3   CAD tools

CAD tools are highly sophisticated computer applications packages, which are highly customised (or customisable) to meet the needs of a particular application or range of applications. In their simplest form, they provide a tool which allows for the production of a diagram representing some part of the design process. An engineer producing the design for a new car might apply a CAD tool on the production of the draughtsman's diagrams of the engine and the chassis. The CAD tool provides, in this instance, the advantages of speed and adaptability, since a small change in the design can be made and the plans can be reprinted without reworking the entire sheet (Figure 5.1).

So CAD tools provide a cost-effective diagrammatic package for use in conventional engineering environments, but it is not just their graphics capabilities which make them important. Most sophisticated CAD tools also provide a *database* of some kind which gives additional functionality. For example, CAD tools used in the design of vehicles for a company typically give access to a database which contains details of all the known components and vehicle parts already in stock and readily available. The design engineer can then call up the database at any point in the design, in order to ascertain whether any existing component which is readily available can be used for a particular part of the design. In this way, the CAD package provides an opportunity to identify occasions where existing expertise, equipment, tools or suppliers can be used in the manufacture of a new design, and this can save millions of pounds in the acquisition and storage of new parts to a different specification when existing components could have been used equally well. Additionally, the CAD tool database contains precise information about the components already available, and allows their use to be tried out on screen. This

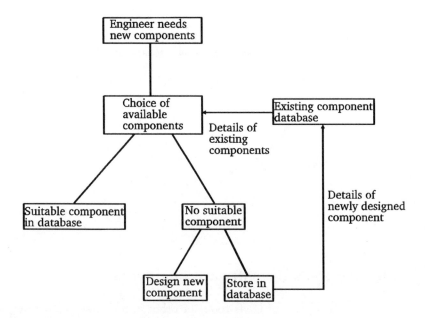

Figure 5.2 The CAD database holds information on available components

can save large sums in the future if adaptations to the design would otherwise need to be made to ensure a comfortable fit (Figure 5.2).

In summary, a CAD system provides the designer with access to information about other designs and components, the ability to try out new designs on screen before printing the plan, the ability to make small changes to a design without redrawing the entire plan, and the facility to check that the parts employed in the design will actually fit together.

Steps further along the road to automation from CAD are represented by Computer Aided Design and Manufacture (CADAM) and Computer Integrated Manufacture (CIM). CADAM and CIM both apply the design produced by computer directly into the production stage of the development and allow the rapid production of prototype models directly from the design. Naturally the sophistication of such systems varies, from the direct production of a particular component by a machine tool which is linked to the designer's computer, to a fully automated production line with many component and subassembly points which can be controlled by the designer's computer to produce the current design (Figure 5.3).

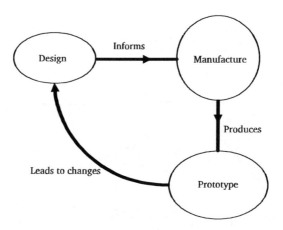

Figure 5.3 CIM system

5.4   Software tools for software engineers

Alongside the developing use of CAD tools for other branches of engineering has been a desire to employ comparable packages in the development of computer software. Here of course the issues are rather different from those in other industries, but there is nevertheless a desire to employ a software tool which offers the same sort of level of functionality as we identified for a sophisticated CAD system in the Section 5.3.

Thus it is our desire to find a computer software package which will actually assist in the design process. This means that the package adopted must be more than just a graphical tool, which alone would permit the preparation of the diagrammatic representations of various stages in the software design or development process, but would still rely on the skills of the software engineer to check that the design was satisfactory. The type of software package which gives similar functionality to the CAD packages needs to be able to hold some sort of database which contains details of the design at various stages and levels of detail. It must allow us to call up the detail from other stages to check consistency. We also desire that the software should help us check whether different parts of the design are consistent with each other, and whether those diagrams which have a known and clear set of rules have been accurately drawn (Figure 5.4).

We therefore follow Gane (1990) in identifying a CASE tool as being a

> (software tool which assists in the software development process and) builds within itself a design database, at a higher level than code statements or physical data element definitions.

Later in the chapter we shall discuss the use of other software tools in the development of computer systems. We shall look at the use of *general* tools which give

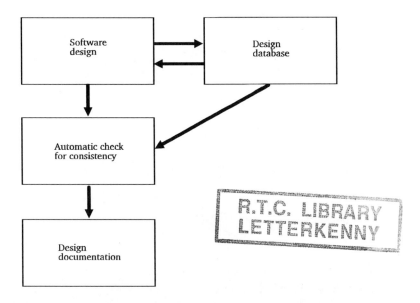

Figure 5.4 Outline of software development using a CASE tool

the opportunity to reproduce some of the aspects of CASE tool use when a CASE tool is not available. We shall also look at other types of specialist tool, which do not conform to our definition of a CASE tool but are nevertheless important in the production of computer software.

5.5   CASE tools and the choice of methodology

One of the principal features of the introduction of software engineering techniques into the development of computer systems is in the introduction of rigorous and clearly defined methods and procedures for the production of the software. As we saw in Chapter 4, different methodologies have been adopted by different organisations and there are now a plethora of different methodologies. We also saw that some different methodologies differ in their level of rigour, some in their approach to solving the software development problem, while others differ in emphasis, in the order and precise type of diagrammatic representations which they employ and in the precise ordering of the stages in software development.

It is not our purpose in this book to favour any particular method, although we have chosen to focus on methods which are appropriate to the SSADM systems analysis strategy. The reason for this is two-fold. First it is the methodology with which we are most familiar, and second because of Governmental policies, it is more widely adopted, at least within the United Kingdom, than other methods.

Nevertheless, the approach and methods which we describe would apply equally

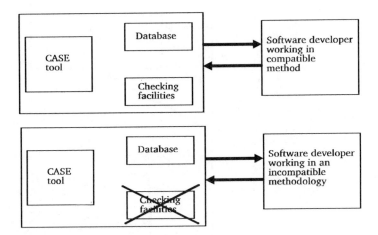

Figure 5.5 It is important that a CASE tool chosen matches the methodology in use, otherwise the checking facilities will be wasted

to users of other rival methodologies.

While the different types of software engineering method are similar in their aims, methods and structure, there are these important differences in order and style of presentation of ideas. It is therefore important to take into account the methodology supported in the acquisition of any CASE tool. Most CASE tools have been designed to suit a particular methodology and therefore provide all the support for working within that. It would often be possible to apply the tool to the use of a rival method, but this would be rather inefficient, since the tool will not necessarily point out errors and inconsistencies in the design in this case. It might also be difficult to produce diagrams to the correct specifications if they are beyond the scope of the drawing tool within the CASE package (Figure 5.5).

We should therefore look for a tool, designed either for the particular methodology adopted, or (and this is probably the more desirable alternative) designed to be used as a *generic* tool but with add-on specific components relating to a range of different methods. In this latter case, there is the advantage that the tool will probably be able to cope in two common scenarios:

1. There may be a need within a particular project to provide additional diagrams beyond those specified by the method in use. This might be because of some particular requirements of the client, or because of some strange feature of the problem. A more general-purpose tool is more likely to be able to cope with these diverse demands.
2. It is surprisingly common for organisations to change their methodology. This happens either because of some staff changes, some bad experience using the previous method, or even the demands of a particular client that a particular

Figure 5.6 Generic customisable CASE tools may be more versatile

methodology is required. It is therefore much more cost effective if a tool is available which can be customised to suit a variety of different methods to avoid both the expense and the retraining cost and resulting delay from having to have employees adapt from a familiar tool to an unfamiliar one (Figure 5.6).

The rapid pace of developments in software engineering methods and in the availability of tools and hardware on which to run them has meant that many users have had to adapt to a number of tools over quite a short time. In addition, some of the early tools were of less value than more recent tools, and this has resulted in some software developers being sceptical of the value of software engineering tools of any kind.

5.6 How do you choose a suitable CASE tool?

Having established the methodology to be used in the software development process and therefore knowing what must be supported by the tool which is to be acquired, how should an organisation go about finding a suitable tool? This is really two problems in one:

1. How do you find a list of all the tools to support a particular methodology?
2. How do you determine the quality, functionality and reliability of the tools available for the chosen method?

Both these questions can be answered by reference to the STARTS publications distributed by the National Computing Centre in the United Kingdom (see Bibliography). These documents give the following:

- A description of software engineering
- A list and brief description of the available methods
- A list of suitable software packages
- An evaluation of each of the packages available.

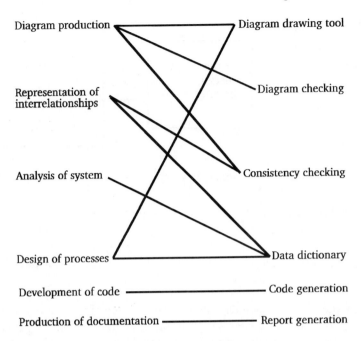

Figure 5.7   Relationship of stages in software engineering and the functions of CASE tools

It therefore becomes a relatively straightforward task to identify two or three appropriate products to investigate further.

5.7   Functionality

We now turn to address, in a little more detail, the question of what a CASE tool can typically undertake. In order to see the range of possible activities and features, we have presented a diagrammatic representation (Figure 5.7).

On the left-hand side of Figure 5.7 are the principal stages in the development of software and its documentation:

1. The production of diagrams to represent different views of the system
2. The representation and understanding of the interrelationships between diagrams and diagram elements
3. The analysis of the data
4. The design of the various processes which will go to make up the final system
5. The development of the program code itself
6. The production of the system documentation.

On the right-hand side are some of the important issues in the production of the software. These include the quality issues, those issues important to management such as the speed and cost of production and the overall project management strategy.

In the central area of the diagram are some of the features of a typical CASE tool which serve the requirements on both sides of the diagram.

5.7.1 The production of diagrams

We have identified a range of diagrams as being important in the software engineering process. Diagrams which we find particularly useful are the data-flow diagram, the document-flow diagram, the entity life history diagram and the Jackson structure diagram. Other software engineers find different diagrams most useful. The important thing from the point of view of the CASE tool is the requirement that it can be used to produce each of the necessary types of diagram.

This means, among other things, that the graphical facilities of the tool should allow the production of each of the box shapes and each of the interconnecting links which go to make up each of the diagrams required. This is the most fundamental requirement, and we would really hope that the tool offered further functionality. One feature which is particularly useful is the option to choose a particular diagram type and then to be offered exactly the box and linkage shapes which are permitted within the diagram chosen. Some tools then encourage accurate production of the diagram by allowing reference to the boxes to be by description of the type of information they hold. This, for example, avoids the possibility of putting *process information* in a box designed to hold *data*!

The best tools permit the checking of a diagram once it is complete. The diagram production is subject to a set of rules defined by the methodology, and these can be built in to a checking facility when the tool is produced. Therefore mistakes, such as the use of the wrong type of box in a particular place on the diagram or the omission of an important link, may be found by the tool when the diagram is checked for consistency.

It is useful to be able to perform these consistency checks, but it is important to be clear about their scope and their limitations. Consistency checking does precisely what it says. It checks that what has been represented in the diagram makes sense, but it does not check that it is accurate. Thus, after a data-flow diagram has been checked for consistency, we will know that the resulting diagram is a data-flow diagram, but not if it represents the proposed system faithfully.

When we come to draw diagrams such as data-flow diagrams, it is often useful to be able to represent a system at various levels (see Figures 6.2-6.4 in Chapter 6). Here we can see that the overall structure of the system is best illustrated by the first diagram, which is made clear by the absence of unnecessary detail. However this means that there is not sufficient detail to understand how the system *really* works. Increasing levels of detail, but correspondingly less clarity of the overall

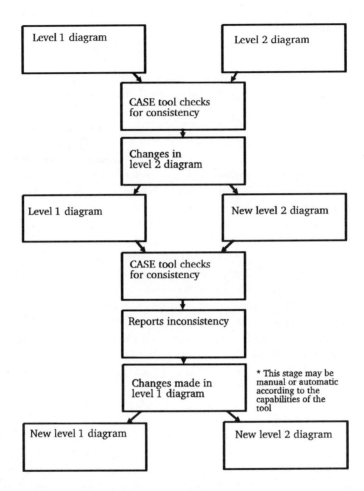

Figure 5.8 The role of a CASE tool in maintaining the consistency of diagrams

picture are provided by the subsequent figures.

CASE tools can typically help in the production of these diagrams by allowing the construction of each greater level of complexity stage by stage from the original simple diagram. This is particularly helpful, since it means that the different diagrams can be stored *linked together*. These diagrams are, after all, only varying levels of detail of the same fundamental diagram, and this link in the way they are stored means that changes made to any diagram within the set can be identified by the CASE tool as necessary in all the linked diagrams. Some tools can undertake the changes automatically in all diagrams. Other tools simply prompt that the diagrams at different levels are no longer consistent and that changes are therefore needed (Figure 5.8).

5.7.2   Holding details of relationships

We know from experience how easy it is to become confused when trying to understand a complex system. We also know how important it is to keep a clear idea about the way in which different aspects of a system interrelate.

For example, if we consider for a moment the representations of a particular system, we might have a data-flow diagram which indicates the way in which data flows between sources and sinks within the system. We might also have a document-flow diagram which indicates the movement of documents between people and departments. Both diagrams can provide useful information. In the one case the focus is on the documents and in the other case the focus is on the data, but apart from that there is a lot of common information in the two representations.

On the other hand, since the two representations are both considered potentially useful, there must be occasions where the one representation provides information not explicit in the other. This is where the establishment of the database of information about the system, to which we referred earlier in this chapter, becomes crucial.

Typically, a CASE tool provides us with a data dictionary or data repository. Again, we follow Gane (1990) in his description:

> (the repository) supports the storage of detail about data structures, data elements and process logic, cross-referenced to the graphical models.

Thus, when we refer to a particular item, such as the order form, in the document-flow diagram, there will be an element in the data dictionary which contains full details about the content of the order form and the way in which it is used. This information will have to be entered on the first occasion that the order form is mentioned. If the order form then appears in a second place, perhaps on a different diagram, the software engineer is prompted that an order form is already known within the data dictionary. At this stage the software engineer has to make a decision. Either the order form referred to here is the same as the one which the data dictionary already contains, in which case the detail about the order form needs to be checked for completeness, or the order form now mentioned is different and needs to have a new title and a new entry in the data dictionary (Figure 5.9). The data dictionary contains details about the data items, data structures, processes and objects within the system.

This means that the data dictionary ensures the following:

1. Only one entity, process or data item is given a particular name. This avoids ambiguity and confusion later.
2. All the references to a particular item are known and held. This allows tracking across different representations of the system to check that changes made are consistently represented in all diagrams.

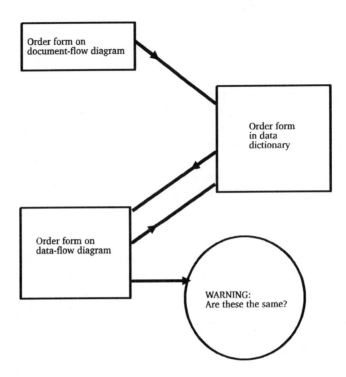

Figure 5.9 The CASE tool checks for ambiguity in the names of objects in different parts of the design

3. All the relevant information about a data item or process are collected at the time when the different parts of the design are constructed. One of the common causes of problem within a system design is when a new part of the system demands changes to an already designed part. Here we are able to ensure that all the material relating to each object is stored together.

5.7.3 The analysis of the data

One of the things which we shall see as important in later chapters is the analysis of the data to help us to find both the most convenient and efficient method of storage. In essence, for most systems, this will involve the production of some sort of database.

A technique for ensuring that a database is designed appropriately and efficiently is known as normalisation. Many CASE tools are capable of taking data structures from the data dictionary and converting them to normal form. Since this is a technique which can also be performed by hand, we shall postpone our detailed discussion of normalisation until later.

5.7.4   Process design

There are two important features of process design. In the first, and the one more commonly thought of under this title, there is the actual design of the suite of programs which will undertake the processing specified for the project. Typically, as we shall discuss later, this involves the stepwise refinement of the problem into a series of smaller problems each of which can be subdivided.

The method of representation we shall normally choose for this technique is the graphical image known as the Jackson structure diagram. CASE tools can usually assist in the production of these structure diagrams or of something similar.

The second feature of process design concerns the design of the user interface. The desire to produce attractive, user-friendly computer software is becoming more significant, and indeed is a requirement for applications in widespread use.

Some CASE tools have reacted to the need to design attractive screen representations by providing *screen painting* and *forms generation* tools within the package. This means that the software designer can work on making the user interface as attractive and appropriate as possible while other aspects of process design are tackled. Therefore the user's need for a good interface with the machine can be built into the design, rather than trying to add it in later (Figure 5.10).

5.7.5   Code generation

For many, perhaps most, software developers and users, the concept of typing the design for a new system into a package which will then generate the necessary program automatically is attractive. There have been several attempts to write packages which will do this, with varying levels of success.

Some CASE tools are provided with a *code generation* section which supports the production of programs in a suitable language from the specification stored in the data dictionary. As with most such attempts, the success of the system is dependent upon the definition being accurate and complete, and on the tool being designed for the appropriate type of application being developed. Typically, the development of code which handles data-processing applications using dBase, SQL or COBOL seems to be the most common satisfactory outcome.

The performance of code written using a code generator is often poor compared with directly written code, and this means that it may be applied more appropriately to the production of prototypes rather than fully working systems. The development of this type of prototype system directly from its specification is a theme of Ford and Ford (1993) (see also Appendix IV).

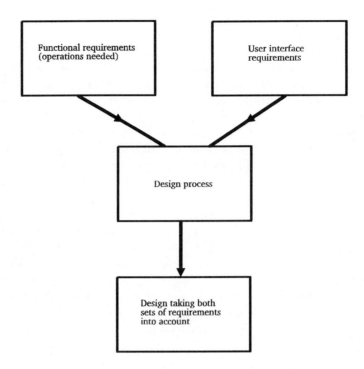

Figure 5.10 The user interface requirements can be designed in

5.7.6   Documentation

The documentation of software projects is a notorious problem to which we have already alluded. Programmers and software engineers tend to be employed because of their technical skills rather than because of their ability (or desire) to write long documents. The result can be that documentation is poorly written, has major omissions and is inconsistent.

Two features of CASE tools help in the documentation process. The establishment of a data dictionary which contains a complete and accurate description of all the data objects and all the processes makes it easier to ensure that any descriptions given are complete and accurate. This avoids many potential problems, but does not solve the problem of motivation!

Fortunately, some CASE tools provide a report generator feature which allows for the establishment of a standard documentation process which can then be selected at will. This means that the majority of the documentation may be produced automatically by the system, which selects the appropriate diagrams and material from the data dictionary. This introduces a standardised format and an increased

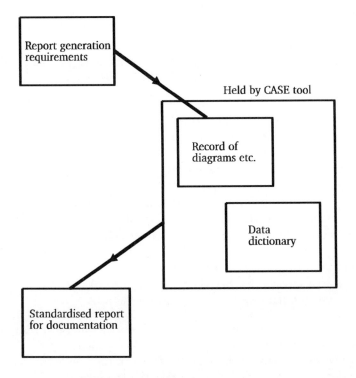

Figure 5.11 Report generation can assist in documentation

likelihood that documentation will be produced, both of which are major factors in improving the software development process (Figure 5.11).

5.8 Other software used in the software engineering process

It can be surprising to discover the range of software used by software developers and which are claimed to benefit the software development process. Obvious examples such as word processors (particularly those which include technical documentation features and diagrams) and desktop publishing packages are named by many designers as being crucial to their production of clear specifications and good documentation. In this section we identify some other software which may be found useful.

One such tool is the **project management** package. We met project planning in Chapter 4 and will discuss issues relating to project management generally in later chapters. Software tools are used to assist in project management in the software industry and elsewhere. Some tools are particularly designed for the software engineering process, and these are described by some authors as CASE tools. We have made the decision to adopt the narrower definition of CASE tools which we gave earlier.

Another significant tool is the Computer Aided Software Testing (CAST) tool. For more information see *Computing* (1992). CAST tools include debuggers, static analysis tools, coverage analysis tools and dynamic analysis tools:

- Debuggers help the developer to locate actual bugs in the program code. These are errors which need to be removed before the program will run and produce the appropriate output.
- Static analysers inspect the code for quality and maintainability. Therefore they measure the number of very complex statements which will be hard to correct and change. They also seek redundant code which is never executed.
- Coverage analysis checks that all the possible routes through the program code have been tested. One possible way of accomplishing this is to use a test data generator which analyses the code, then produces a list of test data which ensures that every possible pathway is thoroughly tested.
- Dynamic analysis checks that the program does what is required and that the software and hardware are sufficient for the task.

The **front-end** package is another interesting item of software which has become important recently. This is a package which provides good easy to use facilities to develop the user-interface of the system. This can then be integrated with the more conventionally written code to undertake the processing.

5.9   Why is CASE a reluctant choice for so many?

The biggest problems with the adoption of CASE are the relatively low quality of the earliest offerings, the difficulty of tool use and the high prices which CASE tools still command. In fact, as the suppliers are eager to point out, the potential savings in time in drafting and redrafting programs and documentation could well justify the cost of purchasing a tool in the first project, but software developers are still sceptical.

It is unfortunate that the cost of CASE packages seems high when compared with other software which is superficially capable of similar functions. The difficulty which CASE tools have in establishing their worth is in convincing the user of the hidden value of the integration of information provided by the data dictionary.

5.10   Advice to students

Throughout the remainder of this book, we have tried to take account of the needs of those students with access to CASE tools. You will find suggestions for activities which will help your understanding of how they can be used. For those readers who do not have access to any CASE tools, there will be some opportunity to undertake similar exercises using more standard software packages (such as CAD or graphics packages).

5.11   Exercises

Self-test questions

1. What is the data dictionary?
2. Why should we not use a simple drawing program and a database instead of an expensive CASE tool?

Exercises

1. What do you think is the most important feature of a CASE tool?
2. If you were a software developer would you buy a CASE tool? Justify your response.

Assignment

Do employers who adopt software engineering techniques also generally use CASE tools?

Chapter 6

Systems analysis: stages and techniques

6.1 Introduction

In this chapter, we give a more detailed description of the systems analysis process. Each stage is described, and the description is complemented by examples from the dentist's scenario introduced in Chapter 4. None of these examples is technical, to ensure that the underlying issues can be readily understood.

6.2 Background

Systems analysis is the first major stage in the system life cycle. According to the approach taken, it may be carried out by one or more professional analysts, or by a design team comprising both analysts and users. The involvement of users in the system development process is one of the ideas we introduced in Chapter 4. For simplicity we will refer to the *analyst* to mean any member of the team performing the analysis.

The aim of the analyst is to understand the current system (if there is one) in sufficient detail to be able to evaluate it and make recommendations for the new system. The sequence outlined in this chapter is based around SSADM Stage 1. However, it has been modified in order to fit in with the software engineering cycle. Thus the stages covered in this chapter are as follows:

1. Identify the Terms of Reference. This places the whole project in its context. It is a statement of the project intent, how it fits in with the company's business plan, with the expected outcome and so on.
2. Conduct a Feasibility Study. Before the project starts it is vital to be as certain as possible that it will succeed. This is part of the role of the feasibility study and involves estimating the time and costs involved. Once the advice has been accepted by management, the analysis can begin.

3. Initiate the Analysis. The analysis needs to be planned. This includes choosing the design team and formulating a top-level representation of the system in order to distribute tasks. This process takes place alongside project management and quality control mechanisms.

4. Investigate the Current System. The processes and data-flows within the current system are analysed. Physical data-flow diagrams are developed at increasing levels of detail.

5. Investigate System Data Structures. The data contained within the current system are analysed. An entity model is constructed.

6. Develop the Problem/Requirements List. The data-flow diagrams and entity models can now be compared and evaluated to identify any problems which currently exist and any improvements which could be included in the new system.

7. Review the Effects of the Investigation. A quality assurance meeting now occurs, where the management and users check and agree the findings of the analysis stage.

The data-flow diagrams, entity model and the problem/requirements lists which result from the process form the input data for the design phase, as we shall see in Chapter 8.

6.3   Terms of reference

When a project of any sort is commenced, it is important that all the parties concerned are agreed upon the likely costs, time-scale and project outcomes. This avoids any disagreement or confusion later in the life cycle. The *initial* terms of reference focus upon undertaking a feasibility study. The following is an (imaginary) example of some initial terms of reference:

> The aim of the project is to automate and eliminate as far as possible the large amount of paper work involved in the daily running of Drill's Dental Surgery. This is consistent with Section 4.5 of the Business Plan, which states: *We aim to produce an efficient and professional environment for both employees and patients.*
> The feasibility stage of the project will be undertaken by one analyst: Jeremy Jones from Futures Computer Services and will last one month. The report will be available by 6th Sept. 1993 and an oral presentation will be given on the 20th Sept. 1993 (Flynn 1992).

Once the feasibility study has been completed and more detailed objectives agreed upon, the terms of reference can become more detailed and refer to the whole of the system development life cycle.

6.4 Feasibility study

The goal of the feasibility study is to determine whether the project objectives are realistic. This is important to avoid the project going over budget or over time, since this is expensive and embarrassing.

In order to determine whether the objectives are realistic, it is necessary to anticipate the complexity of the system development task. The following are some of the issues which the analyst will need to consider:

- Is the solution likely to be technically feasible? Computer systems have physical constraints, such as their processor speed and the amount of storage which can be accessed rapidly.
- Is the solution likely to be accepted by the employees? Introducing a new system can alter working practices in a manner which is believed to degrade employees' working conditions; there could then be resistance to such a move. Some sort of *impact analysis* will need to be performed.
- How expensive is the whole project likely to be? This is very difficult to estimate and needs to be based on knowledge of previous projects and an understanding of the characteristics of this particular situation. This will be followed by a cost/benefit analysis to establish whether the likely benefits of the system warrant the expenditure.

Answering these questions requires a detailed consideration of the whole project. Thus the analyst may need to perform an initial analysis and design of the system. It may even be necessary to implement a prototype of the design to test on potential users. This is known as a two-pass approach. The initial pass will allow us to develop a system which will give a better understanding of the problem's complexity. The findings can be recorded in detail, in order to provide background information for the second pass when the real working system is being developed.

It is likely that a number of potential solutions will be identified. Each of these will have different advantages and disadvantages. Thus the analyst will need to establish the criteria for comparison. These will usually be based on factors such as cost, acceptability and technical viability. The ultimate decision over these matters is the responsibility of the company management.

The feasibility study in SSADM has numerous stages and it is inappropriate to go into detail here. The approach is to undertake a first pass of stages 1-3 of the SSADM life cycle which we met in Chapter 4. Only part of the process is completed, but this is done in sufficient detail to anticipate likely problems, and identify different technical options so that provisional costings can be made. The usual SSADM techniques, based upon data-flow diagrams and entity models, are used. Examples are given later in this chapter.

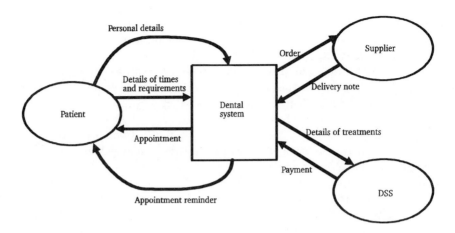

Figure 6.1 Context diagram

6.5   Initiate analysis

Once the feasibility study has been completed and agreed upon, the main analysis can be carried out. It is necessary to ensure that the detailed analysis will be carried out in a consistent and professional manner. This is particularly important for a project carried out by a *team* of analysts, when it will be necessary to ensure that the scope of each analyst's responsibilities is clear and that they are all working to the same standards. This is the objective of the **initiate analysis** stage.

In order to distribute the tasks it is necessary to be aware of the overall structure of the problem. This will already have been identified in the feasibility study. Thus there may be information such as the following available:

> The end product will be in two sections. The first section will be the computerisation of the new patients' booking system (currently manual). This will be achieved by creating a database of all the patients, producing appointment cards and updating the records where necessary. The second section will be the computerisation of the dentist's accounting procedures (Flynn, 1992).

This type of description would be augmented by a context diagram and a level 1 data-flow diagram as illustrated in Figures 6.1 and 6.2. The symbols used in these diagrams were defined in Chapter 4. The diagrams can be interpreted as follows.

The context diagram places the whole system in context. There are transactions with the following external entities: patients, suppliers of dental equipment and the Department of Social Security (DSS). The nature of these transactions varies:

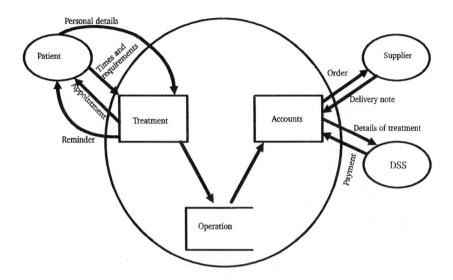

Figure 6.2 Level 1 data-flow diagram

- The patient gives information, and receives appointment details and an appointment card in return
- Orders are placed with suppliers for additional stock and delivery notes are returned
- Treatment details are sent to the DSS, who then pay for the treatment.

The level 1 data-flow diagram illustrates the dentist's system as two main processes:

- Treatment
- Accounts.

These processes reflect the two sections indicated in the text. As expected, the same data-flows exist between the dentist's system and the external entities we saw previously. The only difference is that they now cross the boundary and link to one of the component processes. Thus, dealings with the DSS are handled exclusively by the *accounts* process, whereas dealing with the patients is handled by the *treatment* process. It would be unusual if the processes were not linked in some way. This might be by one or more data-flows or by access to common data stores. In this example, there is a common data store: **operation**. Operation contains details about the various treatments which have been given. These are analysed at regular intervals by the accounts process, so they can be sent to the DSS for payment.

With this level of understanding, the analysis team members can be grouped according to the main processes in the level 1 data-flow diagram. They will need

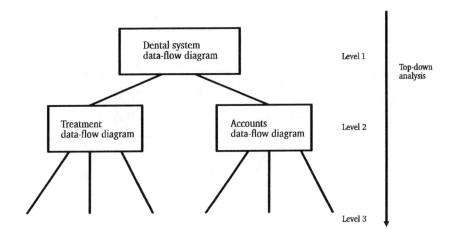

Figure 6.3 Hierarchy of data-flow diagrams

to meet regularly in order to agree upon standards. One issue highlighted by the data-flow diagram is the data passed between these processes, and the way these are to be represented and stored will need agreement. Team members will also need to agree upon the documentation and programming standards. In SSADM the documentation standards are specified in detail.

6.6 Investigate current system

The objective of this stage is to gain a detailed understanding of the processes involved in the current system and the data which flow between them.

The outcome of the investigation will be a number of physical data-flow diagrams at different levels of detail. The development of these occurs as follows:

1. Each process in the level 1 data-flow diagram is used to produce a level 2 data-flow diagram. Thus we would have two level 2 data-flow diagrams for the present example.
2. Each process in the level 2 diagrams would then be used to produce a level 3 diagram, and so on.

We would end up with a hierarchy of data-flow diagrams, as illustrated in Figure 6.3. This process is known as top-down analysis, since we start with a general understanding and this understanding becomes increasingly detailed as the analysis progresses. The number of levels which need to be generated depends upon the complexity of the system. Typically two or three levels are sufficient.

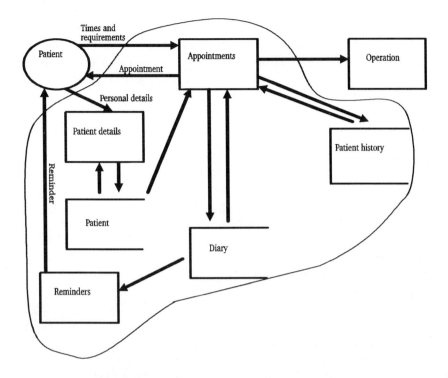

Figure 6.4 Level 2 data-flow diagram: Treatment

To illustrate this, the *treatment* process has been expanded to produce the level 2 data-flow diagram illustrated in Figure 6.4. The meaning of this diagram is as follows.

The treatment process is made up of three processes: patient details, appointments and reminders. *Patient details* is responsible for maintaining an accurate record of patient details. This involves registering new patients and altering their details when it is appropriate. The details are stored in the *patient data store*. This data store was not included in the level 0 diagram as it is only referenced within the treatment process. The *appointments* and *reminders* processes are responsible for registering appointments and generating reminders, respectively. Two other data stores have also been added: *diary,* which contains details of the appointments, and *patient history,* which records the various treatments which each patient has undergone.

As with the transition between the context diagram and the level 1 data-flow diagram, the same data-flows exist between the treatment process and the external elements. The only difference is that the data-flows now cross the boundary and are linked to the internal processes.

The development of data-flow diagrams requires practice. The major difficulty tends to be knowing how much detail to put in each level. In extreme cases, there is a temptation to produce a single detailed data-flow diagram which represents the whole system. The problem with this approach is that it would be easy to get confused and to introduce errors. Using the top-down method, errors within the system are more easily detected at one level than another. For example, in the level 1 data-flow diagram, it can be seen that neither process handles liaison with the local doctor's surgery. This is a separate area and would require a third process.

It is a good idea to adopt a fairly fluid and intuitive process when drawing up data-flow diagrams. Thus the analyst might find that while producing a level 2 diagram, an error in the level 1 diagram is highlighted. This also demonstrates the quality control benefits of top-down analysis.

If a number of analysts draw up data-flow diagrams for the same system, the diagrams may contain differences. Significant differences are usually the result of inadequate fact finding and the discrepancies can help focus on the necessary additional research.

Any problems with the system detected at this stage are added to the problems/requirements list.

6.7   Investigate system data structures

The objective of this stage is to gain a detailed understanding of the data necessary for the current system. This stage is usually shorter than the previous one, as an overview entity model will have been developed during the feasibility study. As a result, much of what is described here actually often occurs earlier in the life cycle.

The outcome of investigating the system data structures is a single entity model, which gives a clear overview of the data and the relationships within the data in the current system. Figure 6.5 is an example entity model for the dentist's system. This diagram can be interpreted as follows.

There are seven entities:

- Patient: contains the name, address and status of the patient
- Patient history: contains a record of the patient's treatment
- Operation: contains a record of the treatment carried out over a period of time
- Operation type: lists the type of operation available
- Appointment: contains the appointment details
- Appointment time: lists the times when appointments can be made
- Appointment type: lists the types of appointment available.

These seven categories of information are currently stored within the system. The nature of the storage will vary. For example, Diary may actually be a diary, whilst Patient would probably be files in a filing cabinet.

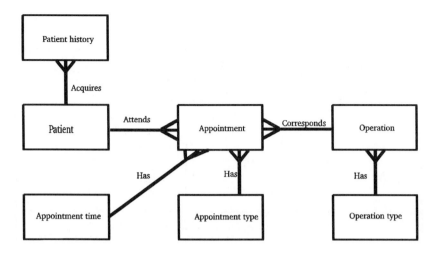

Figure 6.5 Entity model

The entities are linked together as necessary by relationships. The relationships are given in two parts which explain the relationship in one direction and then in the other. The entity which is being started from is always in the singular.

The relationship between patient and appointment means *each patient attends a number of appointments and each appointment is attended by only one patient.*

The relationship between appointment time and appointment means *there can be several appointments at each appointment time (if we assume more than one dentist) and each appointment can only be at one time.*

It can be useful to remember that *entities* often correspond to nouns in the system description and the *relationships* correspond to verbs. Thus in the expression: *the patient attends an appointment,* the entities are: patient and appointment and the relationship is attends. In some conventions, the relationship links are labelled and in others not.

It is important to understand the relationship between the data-flow diagrams and the entity model. The data stores in the data-flow diagram and the entities are related, but this relationship may not be 1:1. For example, the diary data store in the treatment data-flow diagram corresponds to the entities: appointment, appointment time and appointment type. This relationship is illustrated in Figure 6.6.

The relationship between the data stores and entities needs to be checked and monitored by the analysts since this is an effective way of ensuring the correctness and consistency of the two types of diagram.

Once the entity model has been developed, a description of each entity can be derived. This will typically include a list of all the entity attributes. Thus we might have:

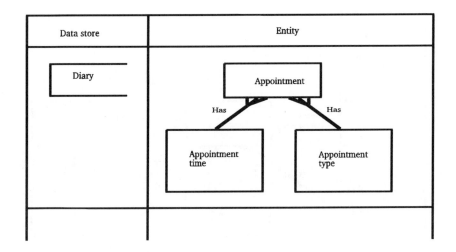

Figure 6.6 Cross-referencing data stores and entities

Patient Entity

- Name
- Address
- Home phone number
- Work phone number
- Age (if under 18).

These entity descriptions are put into a data dictionary, whether a CASE tool is in use or not.

Any problems with the system which are detected at this stage are included in the problems/requirements list.

6.8   Developing the problem/requirements list

The feasibility study, followed by the completion of the data-flow diagrams and entity model, will have produced a list of the problems with the current system and the particular requirements of the new system.

These problems may take a number of forms. In the example discussed in this chapter, we might identify the following:

1. The operation *data store* is currently implemented by adding information to a file in the filing cabinet and the dentist occasionally forgets to record the details of the operation. Thus, the money for the operation is not recovered. This type of error may come to light through the discussion based around the data-flow diagrams.

2. The *patient* entity may need an additional attribute *title*, in order to allow for the generation of address labels. This type of omission may come to light when producing the data dictionary.
3. The current method of implementing the entities may be questioned. For example, if the *patient* entity was implemented using a database rather than as a collection of forms, it could be used for the automatic generation of reminder letters. This type of weakness could come to light when producing the entity model.

Other problems might also be uncovered, such as confusion over the allocation of tasks between members of the organisation, problems associated with the legislation concerning dental practices and environmental issues, such as the problem of being situated on a main road. These problems may not all be resolved by the new system, but identifying them will allow the organisation to take them into account in their strategic plan.

The problems identified will need to be discussed and from these, the requirements for the new system derived. The problem numbered 1 (above) could be avoided by having a computer system, with an appointments database and an operations database which are automatically cross-checked at the end of the day, to ensure that all the operations have been recorded. Any omission will be highlighted. This feature could then be a requirement of any new system.

Additional requirements may also result from the various informal discussions. For example, the dentist, may feel that it is important to be able to book appointments up to 12 months ahead or may wish to have a payment reminder option, for patients who owe money. Some of these requirements may prove to be unrealistic. For example, it would be useful to have the operation types in a database, so that the treatment type entered in the operations database could be checked. However, there are a great many of these and it is not a realistic proposition.

We have made the assumption in the example that the new system is to be a modified version of the existing system. This will not be the case if the existing system is seriously inadequate for some reason, or if there is no existing system. In these situations, it will not be possible to base the system design on existing diagrams and so it will be necessary to develop completely new diagrams during the design phase.

The problems and requirements will need to be documented in detail and prioritised. This forms the basis of software specification, described in Chapter 7.

6.9   Review the effects of the investigation

The analysis stages are carried out by the analyst in consultation with the organisation's management and the potential system users. Thus, before continuing with the design, it is necessary to agree the findings with the management. This involves a formal review of the data-flow diagrams, entity model, problem/requirements list, data dictionary and other documentation produced by the analysis. The management suggest amendments and the corrected document is *signed off* and authorisation given to continue to the next phase.

6.10   CASE tools

The methods described for undertaking the systems analysis focus largely upon the use of diagrams to represent various aspects of the system under consideration. We have identified the context diagram, the data-flow diagram and the entity model as important within this chapter.

A suitable CASE tool will allow us to produce these diagrams, and will also permit the corresponding entities within the diagrams to be interrelated. Thus, the level 1 data-flow diagram can be developed into level 2 diagrams. The data dictionary entries which correspond to the data and flows on the data-flow diagrams will then give cross-reference to corresponding entries on other diagrams. This forms the basis for the error and consistency checking which the software can undertake.

6.11   Exercises

Self-test questions

1. Why is the feasibility study important?
2. What is the purpose of each of the following diagrams:

    - Context diagram

    - Data-flow diagram

    - Entity model?

3. Why might it be worth using a CASE tool to draw the diagrams rather than drawing them by hand?

Computer-based exercises

If you have access to a suitable CASE tool, work through an example to generate the data dictionary and some related diagrams. *This will give you experience to try the computer-based exercise in Chapter 7.*

Assignment

Using job advertisements for systems analysts, try to make a list of the different methodologies in use among employers. What proportion of employers do not state which methodology they use?

Chapter 7

Software specification

7.1 Introduction

In this chapter we shall consider how the findings of the investigations undertaken in the systems analysis, described in Chapter 6, can be presented in a *formal* way which provides the basis for the systems design and development. For convenience, we shall view the software specification in two sections:

- The requirements definition document
- The requirements specification document.

In practical cases, this division may not be explicit, but it will nevertheless be appropriate to describe the requirements in a way which broadly covers those aspects described here.

7.2 The requirements definition

The first part of the software specification, the requirements definition, collects together information and results from the systems analysis which was described in Chapter 6. The production of the document is a matter of presenting, in an appropriate form, facts and information which have already been determined. In some circumstances, the *systems analysts* may be required to produce a requirements definition as the outcome of the systems analysis. This can have some benefits, since the repetition of tasks required in converting the analyst's own report into the pattern required of the requirements definition is then avoided. On the other hand, the primary reason for the production of the requirements definition document is to give the software engineers the opportunity to reach a clear understanding of the requirements of the system to be developed. There may therefore be advantages in the engineers spending some time working from the analysts' report in producing

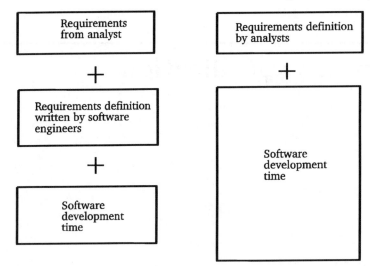

Figure 7.1 Taking more time at the requirements definition stage may reduce total development time in the long run

a requirements definition, which can then be discussed with the analysts. The additional time spent at this stage in coming to a clear understanding of the project to be undertaken may well pay dividends for the engineers in the future (Figure 7.1).

As we shall see, it is in the nature of this document that the methods of presentation of the material in the requirements definition document reflect closely the diagrams used in the systems analysis stage.

7.2.1   The content of a typical requirements definition document

Particular teams of software engineers, company managements and methodologies dictate precisely what should constitute a requirements definition document. The list of contents described here should therefore be considered illustrative rather than prescriptive:

1. *Introduction*

   Most newly developed systems are best understood against some background information. Thus, the introduction may refer to the company or department under consideration and give background information as to why the current project is being undertaken. This introduction will be based upon the material considered by the analysts in the feasibility study, and will highlight any particular needs for the new system. For example, if the overriding consideration in the production of the new system was to improve cash flow by shortening the delay in producing invoices, then this would be stressed appropriately within the introduction to the requirements definition.

2. *System model*

A *model* of the proposed system may often be evident as one output from the systems analysis stage. Different approaches to systems analysis produce diagrams of different types. The approach described would mean that data-flow diagrams, entity models and entity life histories would form the most natural ways of describing the system model diagrammatically.

3. *Functional requirements*

Every system must be used to do something. It is therefore usually helpful to construct a list of the *functional requirements* of the system, which details those things which the system must do. A system which deals with dental appointments might include the following within its list of functional requirements:

F1 A record of appointments is to be maintained.

F2 Reminders are to be produced for patients due for a return visit.

F3 A list is to be produced of patients who fail to attend appointments more than twice.

F4 A sheet of appointments for each day is to be produced for each dentist.

It is helpful to produce a list like this, because it can be shown to the client whose system is being produced and used as a constant record by the software engineers. The list of functional requirements provides an added check that the system model shown in the diagram does indeed complete *all* the necessary tasks.

Sometimes it can be convenient to subdivide some of the functional requirements of the system. The list above might become, for instance:

F1 A record of appointments is to be maintained:

F1.1 Appointments can be added

F1.2 Appointments can be deleted

F1.3 Appointments for a particular patient can be found.

F2 Reminders are to be produced for patients due for a return visit.

F3 A list is to be produced of patients who fail to attend appointments more than twice.

F4 A sheet of appointments for each day is to be produced for each dentist.

4. *Hardware*

The hardware for the desired system will need to be described at this stage. It will be presented to the software engineers as a constraint on their freedom to design the hardware around the system which they develop. This is because, either the hardware to be used will have been presented to the systems analysts as a constraint (for example, because of the desire to use surplus capacity on existing hardware) or else the systems analysts will have needed to budget for the purchase of suitable hardware as part of their estimates for the cost of the project. In either case, the software engineers will have little flexibility to specify changes in the hardware which is to be used.

5. *Database requirements*

   Chapter 6 contained details of how the systems analysts will have analysed the data requirements of the proposed system. This includes the design of suitable database records through techniques such as normalisation. At this point details of the conclusions reached will be recorded in the requirements definition.

6. *Non-functional requirements*

   One of the principal themes of this book, and one of the most important aspects of system development which motivates the use of software engineering techniques is the desire to improve software quality. We describe in Chapter 12 what exactly constitutes high-quality software. One interesting fact is that most users judge the *quality* of the software which they use according to rather vague notions of quality, which do not correspond directly to the functions which the software undertakes. For example, a word-processor will be judged according to how easy it is to use, or how quickly commonly used functions can be accessed, rather than the vast array of facilities available. Therefore the quality of the software, as far as the user is concerned, often focuses on these *non-functional requirements*. Of course, this does not mean that the functionality of the software is unimportant, but rather that the user assumes that the software in question performs the functions expected of it, and also expects a high-quality piece of software to display features such as **speed**, **ease of use** and a **high-quality user interface.**

   Aspects of the requirements which relate to *qualities* of the software rather than functions are listed under the heading non-functional requirements. Failure to satisfy the non-functional requirements of the specification may be seen by some as a less serious failing than failure to meet the functional requirements, but nevertheless non-functional requirements are likely to be crucial to the long-term satisfaction of the user with the system.

7. *Maintenance information*

   Sometimes a newly designed computer system is subject to constraints imposed from outside which are relevant to the design. For example, it could be that a change in legislation is pending, and a new system must therefore be designed in such a way that this change can be incorporated easily in the future. On the other hand, it could be that the life of the system being designed is likely to be far greater than the life of the computer hardware being used. Therefore it would be desirable to ensure that the system designed and implemented would be *portable* to avoid placing too many constraints on the choice of replacement hardware in the future.

Some types of software have a clearly limited life. In this case, the short life needs to be taken into consideration. The longer the potential life of the software, the more appropriate it is to optimise the speed of operation, even if the work involved in doing this is substantial. However, if a program will be used for only a short period, it is more important to complete it quickly and accurately than to worry unduly about its efficiency of operation.

Sometimes it is appropriate to take into account possible mergers and take-overs of the organisation in the design of computer systems. The cost of rewriting a system simply so that it becomes compatible with that of a parent company can be enormous, but may be easily coped with at the design stage as long as this requirement is made known.

The section on maintenance information therefore describes these future requirements of the system in order to enable them to be taken into account by the software engineers when the system is designed and implemented.

8. *Glossary and index*

Finally, within the requirements definition document is an index and glossary. Sometimes it will be necessary for the software engineers to come to terms with the jargon and specialist words which relate to the areas of application. In these cases it is most satisfactory to include a glossary of these words within the definitions document in order to avoid different members of the team reaching a different understanding of the same information.

7.2.2 The purpose of the requirements definition document

The requirements definition document, as described here, is a crucial stage in the project. It marks the point where the investigations into requirements carried out by the systems analysts end and the developmental work of the software engineers begins (see Figure 7.2). Any mistakes within the requirements definition document are likely to be carried forward into the systems specification, the systems design and the final working system.

For some organisations, the requirements definition may be drawn up as part of the contract of employment for the team of software engineers. This can be a very satisfactory arrangement, since it ensures that both sides understand that this is the basis of the agreement to produce a working system and that any changes to the agreed definition will need to be renegotiated in detail.

On the other hand, there can be advantages in having the systems analysts draw up a report on their conclusions, which should then be interpreted into a separate requirements definition document by the software engineers. The added checking this allows is an excellent quality control procedure.

When the system is finally completed, the requirements definition document will form an important part of the system documentation. It will form the basis for quality control checks and testing, since it defines what the system should be able to cope with and identifies the non-functional requirements which should be met.

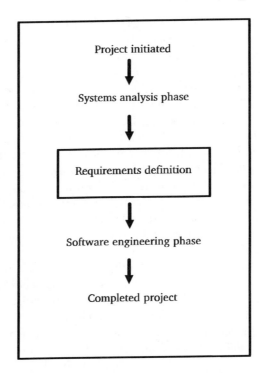

Figure 7.2   The requirements definition lies at the heart of the software development project

Furthermore it will be useful as a definitive reference document for any subsequent systems analysis when the time comes to consider a change to the system.

All these purposes for the requirements definition document can only be realised if the document is accurate. We have already referred to the importance of checking that the definition reflects accurately the needs of the client. Equally important is the requirement that the document accurately reflects the system.

From a purist viewpoint, this last statement should be nonsensical. Clearly the aim should be to design the system so that it completely meets the definitions listed in the requirements definition document, and to check that the requirements definition document describes the required system perfectly before any further developmental work is undertaken. In practice however, it is rarely appropriate to implement the system exactly as defined in the requirements definition. This can be for any of the following reasons:

- An error in the requirements definition is spotted by the software engineer at a later stage in the systems development. For example, it may be that an inconsistency has not been noticed.
- The needs of the organisation might change between the requirements definition being agreed and the system being implemented.

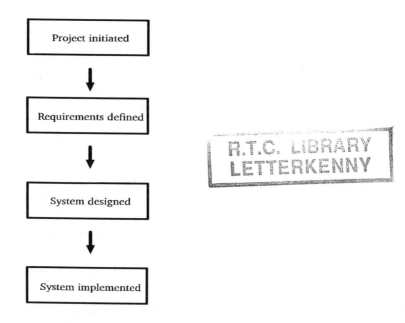

Figure 7.3 Theoretical view of systems development

- There may be implementational reasons why a particular requirement should be changed. (See Figures 7.3 and 7.4.)

Clearly, we should aim to avoid any of these occurrences, since all stem from a failure to employ the desired rigour in producing the definition in the first place. Nevertheless, to pretend that changes to the requirements definition will not occur is to ignore the facts.

As a result of this, the requirements definition document agreed at the start of the software engineer's work should be updated iteratively as the project proceeds. Changes to the agreed document need to be referred both to the client and to the software engineer (and it would often be appropriate to discuss changes with the analysts as well). The agreed amended requirements definition document should then replace the original, and the corresponding changes should be made at every stage of the project between the requirements definition and the stage of development reached. Thus at each stage, all the documentation must be kept consistent with itself and with the evolving system. The scenario illustrated in Figure 7.5 must be avoided.

One advantage in using a CASE tool in the production of software is that changes made at each level in the documentation automatically result in changes being made in the data dictionary, and reports of inconsistencies with documents at every level can be invited by rerunning any analysis options within the tool. Thus the CASE tool can assist the software engineer in keeping track of the ways in which

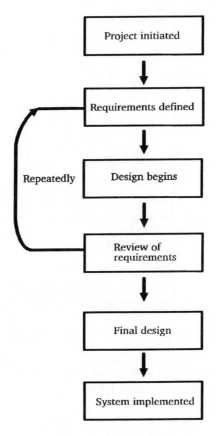

Figure 7.4 More realistic systems development

minor changes at a particular stage in the system design may affect descriptions held elsewhere.

7.2.3   Properties of a good requirements definition document

A good requirements definition is

- Accurate
- Complete
- Clear and unambiguous
- Agreed by client, systems analysts and software engineers
- Implementation independent
- Revised in accordance with every change agreed.

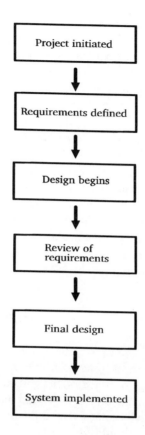

Figure 7.5 An unacceptable approach to systems development

Most of these requirements have been discussed in the preceding section, but the requirement of *implementation independence* is an important one which has not previously arisen in this chapter.

In order to appreciate the importance of implementation independence, we need to focus once again on what the purpose is of the requirements definition. The document provides an agreement for the development of a new computer system, so it describes in detail what must be done by the system and what are the qualities which should be displayed by the completed software. However, it is not the intention of the requirements definition document to instruct the software engineer *how* the software should be designed or written. This decision is quite properly the province of the software engineer, who should consider what is required and the tools and languages available to assist in its delivery.

In Chapters 8 and 9 we discuss the decision which must be taken and the ways in which it may be arrived at. For the present it is sufficient that we see that it is important not to define the requirements *in terms of how they might actually be implemented.* This is rather simpler to state than it is to achieve, since every experienced software engineer will have undertaken projects previously and will develop a particular approach to their solution. It may be very difficult to specify what is required without having in mind at the same time an understanding of what the completed system might look like.

7.3   The requirements specification

The document which we refer to as the requirements specification is an attempt by the software engineer to set out in a more precise way the requirements detailed in the requirements definition. It is a document for use by the software engineer in the subsequent stages of the project, and therefore is not designed with the needs of a more general readership in mind. In particular, technical language and definitions are appropriate in this document, even though they would not be acceptable in the requirements definition because of the wider readership of that section.

7.3.1   The purpose of the requirements specification

The specification in an unambiguous form of precisely what the completed system will do is both crucial to the development of high-quality computer software and one of the major shortcomings of much of the software developed. The problem relates to the information which is being expressed and the language which must be used to express it. Thus it becomes very difficult to give a description which satisfies the constraints that it should be:

- Accurate
- Complete
- Clear and unambiguous
- Implementation independent.

And yet this is precisely what a requirements specification document must be. A careful clear statement must be given of each of the functions of the proposed computer system, alongside precise details of how *data structures* within the system are to be processed.

Provided we succeed in producing a really good requirements specification document which satisfies all of these properties, then it becomes possible to introduce two quality control procedures, based upon the requirements specification. These are:

- Requirements validation
- Software verification.

We shall discuss these methods in Chapter 12.

7.4 Approaches to requirements specification

In essence, the content of the requirements specification is easy to describe:

- We need a collection of descriptions of each of the tasks to be undertaken by the software, giving details of inputs, processing and outputs.
- We also need details of the data which are to be stored, including details of the data structures which are to be used to store them.
- In addition, all these descriptions must be:

    1. Clear

    2. Unambiguous

    3. Implementation independent.

Different approaches to the presentation of the requirements specification documents have been adopted by software engineers. We shall consider here three of the most important.

7.4.1 Natural language specification

From the human point of view, the use of *natural language* is the most usual way to begin a description. In this case, a language such as English is used to give the descriptions. Earlier on in this chapter, English was used to list some of the functional requirements of a dentist's appointments system:

F1 A record of appointments is to be maintained:

    F1.1 Appointments can be added

    F1.2 Appointments can be deleted

    F1.3 Appointments for a particular patient can be found.

F2 Reminders are to be produced for patients due for a return visit.

F3 A list is to be produced of patients who fail to attend appointments more than twice.

F4 A sheet of appointments for each day is to be produced for each dentist.

Looking at this list, alongside some general knowledge of how a dentist's surgery operates, the reader can begin to gain a view of what these functional requirements are describing. Further levels of detail could be introduced by the refinement of the requirements listed into successively more subdivisions.

This use of natural language is attractive because:

- It uses the software engineer's existing knowledge of language
- It allows ideas to be communicated in a way which is understood by the general reader

- It has the advantage that it makes no attempt to prescribe a method of implementation.

Unfortunately, there is a major drawback in the use of natural languages. This is the fact that natural languages become **ambiguous** in use, open to interpretation by different people in the light of their own experiences. This was evident in the statement above, where the words *alongside some general knowledge of how a dentist's surgery operates* indicate that there is something about this specification of the functional requirements which relies upon the reader having the same general understanding of the way dentist's surgeries operate as the person who wrote the specification.

This might sound like a trivial criticism, but it is in fact very important. It is very difficult indeed to use natural language in specifying a system without leaving open the possibility of either ambiguity or misinterpretation by a reader with different experience or background. The problem is that the writer uses words which are then interpreted differently by the reader. A particular feature of a system under development might be so obvious that nobody bothers to write it down, the need for it is commonly understood by all the members of the team. As a result it can be missed off the specification and never implemented. Thus the use of informal natural language methods of specifying the requirements for a system is fraught with dangers.

7.4.2 Specifications based upon high-level languages

In order to get away from the problems of a totally informal specification system based around a natural language, one approach which can be adopted to good effect is to rephrase the specifications in a language based upon a high-level programming language. Thus pseudo-Pascal or ADA might be used in an attempt to describe clearly what the requirements of the system are. In theory, at least, the use of these languages can be effective in removing the chances of ambiguity and misinterpretation of the requirements of the system. An example of a simple specification using pseudo-Pascal is shown in Figure 7.6. The major disadvantage of the method is that once the software engineer begins to transfer theoretical ideas into the form of statements relating to a particular high-level language, it becomes impossible to continue to think in an implementation-independent way. Therefore there is the distinct danger that the specification will be written more in terms of how it will be implemented, rather than in terms of what it should deliver.

7.4.3 Specifications using formal methods

This discussion leads us to the conclusion that it would be satisfactory to devise a special way of writing software specifications which avoids ambiguity, is clear and

```
Procedure Patientcharges
    begin
    if patient.type = private then
        begin
        calculate treatment charge
        record against patient record
        produce invoice
        end
    else if patient.type = nhs then
            begin
            calculate treatment charge
            if patient.charge = free then
                begin
                record details for nhs
                                    invoice
                end
        else
            begin
            calculate proportions of
            charge
            record patient charge
            against patient
            record nhs charge for nhs
            invoice
            produce patient invoice
            end
        end
end
```

Figure 7.6 Pseudo-Pascal specification

easy for the software engineer to understand and allows for the expression of ideas in an implementation-independent way. These formal methods of software specification are becoming more and more widely studied and applied, and a detailed account of one of them (the Vienna Development Method (VDM)) can be found in Ford and Ford (1993) or Jones (1990). A rival method, the specification language Z, is also widely used (see, for example, Abrial 1980). Appendix I of this book contains a brief introduction to VDM which illustrates some simple applications.

The advantages of using a formal method are clarity, unambiguity, implementation independence and completeness of the specification, but must be balanced against the overhead of having to learn a new language for software specification. The existing formal methods are all mathematically based and therefore can prove unattractive to some users. Nevertheless, recent experience suggests that, motivated by the desire to write high-quality software, the challenge of using a formal method for software specification is worth considering even for those who are less mathematically inclined.

An additional advantage which may prove increasingly significant in the future, is the availability of prototyping systems which accept input of a formal specification in a suitable specification language and produce a rapid prototype system. This prototype can assist in requirements validation and this provides a spin-off benefit of the use of a formal method (see, for example Ford and Ford 1993 or Hekmatpour and Ince 1988).

7.5   The role of the CASE tool

Typical CASE tools have a fundamental role to play in the software specification. In particular we can identify the following contributions:

- The production of diagrams
- The checking of diagrams for internal consistency
- The construction of the data dictionary which assists checking for consistency across different parts of the specification
- The generation of code in an appropriate implementation medium as a prototype system.

Thus the CASE tool is available to help with the quality control of the specification, by both checking the consistency of the system described, and by offering a possible method, through code generation, of producing a prototype system to allow for requirements validation.

7.6   Exercise

Note: For this exercise, it is appropriate to use a CASE tool if you have access to one. If not, then you may complete some parts of the exercise by hand.

For the dentist example, concentrating for the present on the appointments system described in this chapter:

1. Choose some appropriate diagrams to represent the requirements definition and represent them using a CASE tool.
2. Build up the data dictionary entries which correspond to the entities represented in your diagrams.
3. Use the consistency checking facilities of the CASE tool to check your work.
4. If available, see whether you can generate the code for a simple prototype system and use your prototype to investigate the correctness of the software specification.

Chapter 8

System design: stages and techniques

8.1   Introduction

By this stage in a software engineering project, the following documents should exist:

- The analysis document, including data-flow diagrams, entity models, entity life histories and the problems/requirements list
- The software specification document.

In this chapter, we describe how the design for the new system is created. The design process may be carried out by one or more professional analysts, or by a design team comprising both analysts and users. For simplicity, we will refer to the term *designer* to represent whoever is involved in formulating the design. The role of the designer is crucial to enable the programmer to produce a correct program first time.

8.2   Stages in system design

There are a number of different approaches which can be taken to producing the system design and the choice of approach depends upon the characteristics of the problem being solved. For example, if a system is being developed to control a chemical factory, a real-time approach would be the most appropriate.

The approach outlined in this chapter is general purpose. As with the analysis phase, we have presented a simplified approach based around SSADM in order to present a clear description of the processes involved in developing a system design.

The stages covered in this chapter are as follows:

1. Data Design. In the analysis stage, the data are represented by an entity model, with more detail being contained in the data dictionary. It is now

necessary to update these representations in order to satisfy the requirements specification. This results in the required entity model and required data dictionary. Part of this process involves comparing the current entity model and data dictionary against the *third normal form* of the data currently used in the system.

2. Logicalising the Data-flow Diagrams. The processes in the existing system are represented by a context diagram, together with a hierarchy of current physical data-flow diagrams. Now the implementational details are removed from the data-flow diagrams to produce a set of current logical data-flow diagrams which represent what the current system does, but not how it does it. These are then modified to satisfy the requirements specification. This procedure results in a set of required logical data-flow diagrams.

3. Process Design. In order to represent all three views of the system, it is necessary to develop entity life histories for each entity in the current system. These histories are updated to ensure that they reflect the required logical data-flow diagrams and the required entity model produced later.

4. Physical Design. This involves the following phases:

   (a) Development of Physical Data-flow Diagrams. Each of the logical processes can be implemented in a number of ways. At this stage, decisions need to be made about the manner of implementation and the corresponding physical data-flow diagrams need to be drawn up. Physical data-flow diagrams represent how the system will carry out the various processes.

   (b) Database Design. The details of the database files now need to be decided upon. Decisions will need to be made about the manner of implementation.

   (c) Generation of Structure Diagrams. In order to move closer to the program level, the required physical data-flow diagrams are translated into Jackson's structure diagrams. In addition to representing the processes, these also represent the fundamental programming constructs: sequence, selection and iteration.

   (d) Production of Pseudocode. The structure diagrams are used to help produce pseudocode and it is relatively straightforward to use the pseudocode as the basis for the implementation phase.

Note: In the situation where there is no existing system or the new system is to be radically different from the existing one, it will be necessary to produce the diagrams for the data and process design stages from scratch.

8.3   Data design

The data design stage has three phases:

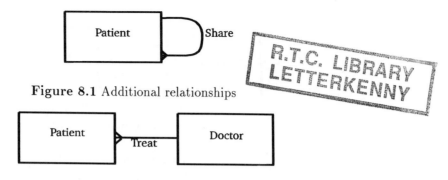

Figure 8.1 Additional relationships

Figure 8.2 Additional entities

1. Modify the entity model and data dictionary
   The modification of the entity model and data dictionary to ensure that they satisfy the requirements specification may involve different types of changes:

   (a) Adding new attributes to the entity. We met the following entity in Chapter 6: Patient entity

   Name
   Address
   Home phone number
   Work phone number
   Age (if under 18).

   The requirements specification may state that it should be possible to generate an address list. One way to achieve this is to implement the patient entity as a database and to add an extra attribute: title, which will contain Mr, Ms, Prof., etc. It would now be possible to generate the complete name and address from the content of the database.

   (b) Adding relationships. If the new system needed to be able to support a mailshot to all patients, it would save postage if the system recorded patients who lived together at the same address. This could be achieved by adding another attribute to the patient entity: groupid. This would contain a unique value for each group of people (typically a family) living at a particular address. This would be illustrated on the entity model as shown in Figure 8.1. We have called the extra relationship *share*.

   (c) Adding entities. If we wish to extend the dentist's system, so that it allows for liaison with local doctor's surgeries, we would need to add an extra entity: *doctor*, to store the necessary details. This would also necessitate the addition of the additional relationship: *treat*. Part of the modified entity model is shown in Figure 8.2.

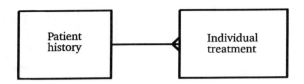

Figure 8.3 Dividing entities

(d) Dividing existing entities. When additional attributes are being added
to an entity or when the entity is being investigated more fully, it may
become apparent that the entity should be divided into more than one
entity. This mirrors the normalisation process which is described later.
For example:

Patient history
Patient id
Operation type
Date
Comments

The *date* attribute may need to contain several dates if the treatment is
ongoing, in which case it would be clearer to divide the entity into two:

Patient history
Patient id
Operation type
Operation no
Comments

Individual Treatment
Operation no
Date
Comments.

Thus each treatment within a course of treatment is represented by the
individual treatment entity. This is clearer and has the added advantage
that comments can be made about each individual treatment and the
whole treatment. Part of the extended entity model is illustrated in
Figure 8.3.

2. Complete relational data analysis

Dentist's table

Patient Name	Patient Address	Distance	Appoint. Time	Appoint. Date	Appoint. Type
Fred Bloggs	10, The Street	Local	10.00 1400	10th Oct 12th Oct	30 mins 15 mins

Figure 8.4 Unnormalised table

Patient table

Patient Id	Patient Name	Patient Address	Distance
p1	Fred Bloggs	10, The Street	Local

Appointment table

Patient Id	Appointment Time	Appoint. Date	Appoint. Type
p1	10.00	10th Oct	30 mins
p1	14.00	12th Oct	15 mins

Figure 8.5 Tables in first normal form

In order to check the revised entity model, it is necessary to develop a bottom-up model of the existing system. In the case of the dentist's surgery, this would involve gathering together all the different forms completed, the reports produced, and anything else which would influence the choice of entities and their attributes. This list might include the appointment card, patient record form, the report sent to the DSS, notes taken by the dentist, the appointment book and so on.

These sources are analysed and compiled into a number of tables. The tables are then transformed into third normal form (3NF). This process is known as normalisation and was developed by Codd (1970). The main advantage of normalised tables is that none of the information is stored in more than one place. Thus there is no redundancy and updating the information is relatively straightforward.

An unnormalised table is shown in Figure 8.4. To transform this into first normal form involves removal of the repeating groups. In the example, Fred Bloggs has several appointments and the fields corresponding to the appointment details are referred to as a repeating group. These correspond to 1:many relationships in entity models.

Thus we can split this table into two tables (Figure 8.5). We have also added a *patient id* field which is the **key field** for the patient table. The key field is the one which uniquely identifies each record in the table. In the

Appointment table

Patient Id	Appoint. Time	Appoint. Date
pl	10.00	10th Oct
pl	14.00	12th Oct

Appointment type table

Appoint. Time	Appoint. Type
10.00	30 mins
14.00	15 mins

Figure 8.6 Tables in second normal form

Patient table

Patient Id	Patient Name	Patient Address
pl	Fred Bloggs	10, The Street

Distance table

Patient Address	Distance
10, The Street	Local

Figure 8.7 Tables in third normal form

example, *patient id* also provides the link with the appointment table.

The key in the appointment table is made up of two fields: *Appoint.Time* and *Appoint.Date*. In order to transform this into second normal form, it is necessary for all non-key elements to be dependent on the whole of the key. In this example, the appointment type is only dependent upon the appointment time. This is because all morning appointments are 30 minutes and all afternoon appointments are 15 minutes. Thus we need to split the Appointment table again (Figure 8.6).

It should be noted that the patient table is already in second normal form, as there is only one key field.

To transform the tables into third normal form, it is necessary to remove any dependencies between non-key elements in each table. In this example, the patient table has a dependency of this type, because the distance field (which indicates if the patient is local or travels from a distance) is entirely dependent upon the address field. Thus the patient table can be split as in Figure 8.7.

This type of dependency exists in no other table and so they are already in third normal form.

3. Create detailed logical data design

We now have the normalised tables, which reflect the operation of the current system and were developed in a bottom-up manner. We also have the entity model, and the data dictionary which were developed in a top-down manner and reflect what the new system should be doing. Thus we are now in a position to compare these in order to detect any inconsistencies.

The types of inconsistency will vary. For example, the entity model may contain additional entities, not represented by the normalised tables. Also the tables may contain fields omitted from the data dictionary entries associated with the relevant entity description. Thus the two representations can be cross-referenced and the entity model and data dictionary corrected.

In addition to correctness, it is important that the resulting data representation should take into account potential developments in the new system. All systems will change over a period of time and the designer should try to anticipate these by making the data representation as flexible and powerful as possible. It has been found that if the data design is of a high standard, the addition of further system facilities is relatively straightforward.

8.4   Logical data-flow diagrams

During the analysis phase, we developed a hierarchy of physical data-flow diagrams which represented the operation of the current system. As with the data representation, we now need to modify these data-flow diagrams, so that they satisfy the requirements specification.

This can be achieved most easily by separating the two central issues: what the current system does and how it does it. Thus we need to start by converting the data-flow diagrams into logical form. This can be achieved in four steps:

(a) Logicalise the data-flows

It is very common for data-flows to be labelled in a physical way. For example, *appointment card* indicates not only that the appointment details are being transferred, but that they are being transferred on a card. The implementational details can be removed by simply using the word *appointment*.

(b) Remove physical time dependencies

Some data stores will have been added because of timing constraints within the existing physical system. For example, if the new patient cards are stored in an in-tray so they can all be filed at the end of the day, this data store only exists because it is more efficient, given the time available to the receptionist. Data stores of this type should be removed.

(c) Logicalise the processes

As with the second phase, some processes might only be necessary because of the manner in which the current system is implemented. For example, the process of collecting and sorting all the new patient cards stored in the in-tray only exists because of the physical implementation of the system. Processes of this sort can be removed. Other processes may need to be renamed to remove the physical aspects. For example, the process *complete appointment card* might be rewritten as *record appointment*. This removes the reference to the appointment card and 'record' is a process which can be carried out in a number of different ways.

(d) Logicalise the data stores

Finally, it is necessary to logicalise the data stores. For example, *diary* may be renamed *appointment*, as the former suggests an actual diary which contains appointments, but the latter does not imply a method of implementation.

It is now possible to see what the current system does and compare this against the requirements specification. Any omissions can be detected and any superfluous stages recognised. This may result in the addition of further processes, data-flows or data stores which may impact upon the data representation, resulting in further alterations to the required entity model. On the other hand, processes, data-flows or data stores may be modified or deleted.

8.5 Process design

We now need to consider the third system view: the event view. This is typified by the entity life history which was introduced in Chapter 4. It is necessary to create an entity life history for each entity. This records the different events which alter the entity in some way. There will be an event which results in the entity being created and others which alter it and one which causes it to be destroyed. Thus the patient entity will be created by the patient registering, it will be altered if he or she moves house locally and it will be destroyed when the patient leaves the area completely.

Each event will be the consequence of a process or a source/sink operating upon a data store in a data-flow diagram. This data store will then cross-reference with one or more entities in the entity model.

Once we have a set of entity life histories for the current system, it is necessary to update these so they are consistent with the data representation and the required logical data-flow diagrams. This updating might involve altering events in the entity life histories and creating new histories for recently added entities. This exercise also acts as a useful cross-reference between the required logical data-flow diagrams and the data representation. At the end of this stage we have a complete *logical* model of the required system.

8.6 Physical design

This is the final stage in the SSADM life cycle. Its outcome is the physical design of the required system. This is made up of two main parts:

- Data design: this forms the basis of the database (or file) design in the resulting program.
- Program specifications: these provide the programmers with unambiguous specifications for the different programs which need to be written to support the database files.

In SSADM the data design occurs first, followed by the program specification, with the development of the program specifications being dealt with in a single step. In this chapter we have rearranged these stages as follows:

Development of physical data-flow diagrams
Database design
Generation of structure diagrams
Production of pseudocode.

We have moved away from SSADM at this point because there is a dilemma: SSADM is a data-oriented design methodology and software engineering is traditionally process-oriented. In other words SSADM considers the data to be central to the system, analyses this first, then identifies the processes needed to support it. In contrast, software engineering considers the processes to be central and so analyses these first and then considers the data. Over recent years, software engineering has become less process-oriented, acknowledging alternative approaches, such as data-oriented design, object-oriented design and real-time design. However, the process-oriented approach is still characteristic and it is this one which we will be describing. It has the added advantages of being well-tested and more detailed than the equivalent phase in SSADM.

8.6.1 Development of physical data-flow diagrams

Earlier in this chapter, we described the process of logicalising the current physical data-flow diagram. This process allowed us to separate the implementational issues from the implementation-independent ones. In other words, it allowed us to consider *what the current system does* to help us make necessary changes. It is now necessary to consider once again how these can best be achieved.

Thus it is necessary to decide upon the following:

- How the processes will be executed. Should they be executed manually or automatically?
- How the data will be stored. Each entity may be stored in a physical container, such as an in-tray, or in a computerised container, such as a database.
- The form in which the data will be transferred around the system. The traditional method of communicating information is the report or memo, but with the use of computers there are alternatives, such as electronic mail or directly updating the relevant database files.

For each of these decisions there may be a number of alternatives, each with associated advantages and disadvantages. The following are some of the issues which need to be considered:

- Time: the time taken to implement the new system. If a manual system is to be completely computerised, this will take more time than a minor modification to the existing system, which may be equally effective.
- Cost: it may be cheaper in the short-term to computerise part of the system. However, in the long-term it may be cheaper to computerise the whole system.
- Physical constraints: if the organisation deals with many thousands of database records, the currently available hardware may be too slow, causing unacceptable delays.
- Organisational constraints: computerisation often affects not only the level of staffing within the organisation, but the types of job which employees carry out. For a new system to be successful, the needs of existing employees for retraining must be taken into account.

It is the responsibility of management to take all these factors into account and decide upon the most appropriate form of implementation. The outcome of this process will be a hierarchy of required physical data-flow diagrams.

8.6.2   Database design

We now have the required physical data-flow diagrams and the data representation, so we can now develop a detailed database design. As with the previous stage there are different ways of implementing the data representation. For example, we may choose to write a program which uses sequential data files. Alternatively we may use a relational database. The approach taken to developing the design depends upon the implementation method.

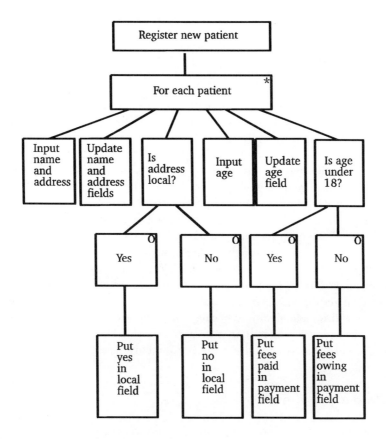

Figure 8.8 Structure diagram

8.6.3   Generation of structure diagrams

The physical data-flow diagrams contain no information about the following issues:

- The sequence in which the processes should be executed
- Which processes are repeated
- Which processes are alternatives to one another.

This information is important when the programming section of the life cycle is reached. The simplest way of representing it is by translating the data-flow diagrams into Jackson's structure diagrams. The syntax of structure diagrams is the same as for entity life histories, but the meaning is quite different

Figure 8.8 illustrates a structure diagram with the following meaning.

The *register new patient* process is made up of the following operations. For each new patient:

Input name and address
Add to name and address fields
If the address is local then put 'yes' in local field
Otherwise put 'No' in local field
Input age
Add to age field
If age is less than 18, put 'fees paid' in payment field
otherwise put 'fees owing' in payment field.

For simplicity, the diagram refers to operations which are all to be performed by a computer. In principle, manual procedures could also be included and these might then be written up in a book of procedures for employees of the company.

Developing a structure diagram involves specifying the program in increasing levels of detail. Thus each higher level operations is subdivided into a number of operations which describe the original operation in more detail. This is a continuation of the top-down design process, which previously produced the hierarchy of data-flow diagrams. The structure diagrams are initially based upon the required physical data-flow diagrams, but as they are expanded, it is likely that new elements will be added simply because they represent a more detailed design. Throughout this development it is necessary to cross-check with the entity life histories to ensure that the requirements specified are being enforced.

8.6.4   Production of pseudocode

We are now getting quite close to code level. The structure diagrams contain the basic programming elements of sequence, selection and iteration. So it is simply a matter of re-expressing the information in programming terms. Typically pseudocode, which we have met already in the context of specification media, is used for this purpose.

There are numerous variants on pseudocode. However, most use a Pascal-type language with constructs such as
WHILE..DO, IF..THEN..ELSE and BEGIN..END.
These are augmented by English descriptions which describe parts of the program which have not yet been fully expanded.

8.7   CASE tools

As we have seen, much of the design phase of the software development continues to apply methods and diagrams which we have already met. In the same way, CASE tools continue to provide facilities for drawing diagrams and checking consistency through the data dictionary. The diagrams which are important to us at this stage are the data-flow diagram, which can appear as a physical or a logical representation of requirements, the entity model and the entity life history and the Jackson's structure diagram.

The second significant feature of CASE tools which is important in this stage in the software development is the normalisation option. Many CASE tools offer the user the option of typing in data structures and providing the third normal form as output.

8.8 Exercises

Self-test question

Why is the software design crucial to the development of high-quality software?

Exercises

1. What is the advantage of normalising data structures?
2. Why may the physical data-flow diagram differ from the logical data-flow diagram?

Assignment

Extend your work from the exercise in Chapter 7. Try to complete a suitable physical design for the software, described both using data-flow diagrams and Jackson's structure diagrams.

Chapter 9

Software implementation

9.1 Introduction

By this stage in a software engineering project, we may assume that:

1. A set of requirements has been defined
2. A more detailed and formal specification of requirements has been given
3. A suitable computerised system has been designed.

This chapter is concerned with how the system specified and designed in these earlier stages of the software engineering process is actually brought into existence. We are therefore concerned with:

1. The choice of the 'mode' of implementation
2. The selection of an appropriate strategy for implementation
3. Checking that the system which has been implemented is a 'correct' system.

Chapter 10 is concerned with the actual techniques of producing the program code.

9.2 Selecting the 'mode' of implementation

If you read conventional books on systems analysis or on software engineering, at this stage it will be assumed that, having designed the programs which are needed, the next task is to choose a suitable programming language and to begin writing the programs.

In this work, however, we have chosen to begin this section by posing a question which we believe to be important:

Having specified and designed the system which we actually want, is writing computer programs the best way of bringing the design into existence?

101

The answer to this question is not particularly easy to determine, but in order to reach some decision, it is necessary for the software engineer to consider the four different modes of implementation currently available and judge each against its advantages and disadvantages.

In order to set the discussion against a concrete example, let us assume that the intention is to provide a new system for computerising a public library.

There are four possible strategies for providing a computerised library system:

- Purchase a specialised computerised library system applications package
- Use a generic software package
- Program using a conventional high-level language
- Generate the software using a fourth generation language (4GL) or code generator.

In the sections which follow, we shall explore each of these possibilities and identify their strengths and weaknesses.

9.3   Purchase a specialised computer applications package

Software is now widely available which can undertake most routine computer-solvable tasks. Computerising a public library is a sufficiently standard task that there are several companies offering purpose-designed software which will actually provide a computerised library facility.

There are a number of advantages of adopting ready-made software of this type:

- The software is available already, so there is a minimum delay between ordering the software and having the new system working.
- The software can be seen working now. There is no chance that software is promised but not delivered on time, because it can be seen and tested.
- The software provides for all the standard needs of a library system. Systems analysts and software engineers will no doubt have been employed on the project and will have considered the requirements of various users in some detail before reaching the specification of the package developed for sale. Therefore, we can probably assume that the package on offer is fairly appropriate to typical needs.
- The cost of ready-written software is often cheaper than the comparable cost of alternative development strategies if staff costs for software development time is taken into account.

However, there are also a number of disadvantages of buying a ready-made solution:

- The principal problem is of a loss of flexibility. The aim from the start of a software engineering project is that we should come to a clear idea of exactly what it is that the system is required to deliver, and how it should perform. If a package is selected, it is important to ensure that the package chosen does indeed perform in accordance with the aims specified previously. No doubt adoption of a package might cause a re-evaluation of some of the requirements listed earlier (for example, does the fact that a package can be made available at lower cost and sooner influence in any way the requirements listed? In addition, does the added assurance that a package will run reliably influence the specification?) However, it is essential that software engineers considering a packaged solution should identify the limitations which a package imposes on satisfying the requirements and renegotiate the requirements definition with the client if necessary.
- A second problem is that packages may be designed for particular hardware which may not be the set-up suggested in the requirements definition. How great a problem this will turn out to be depends largely upon how large a change is needed in hardware specification, and whether the original definition of hardware constraints was based upon a budget, or upon a desire to use existing resources.

9.4   Use a generic software package

If a specialised package is insufficiently flexible for the application which we are considering, then the next option to consider is the use of a generic software package. Generic software packages are pieces of software which have been developed to cater for a particular sort of application, but which have not been configured already to undertake any particular application.

The most well-known generic application, and one which has the most well-defined applications, is the database package. Many readers will be familiar with database packages such as dBase or Dataease. These applications software packages are designed to make it comparatively easy to set up particular sorts of systems based upon the need to store, retrieve and process data in fairly standard ways.

Database packages usually come complete with standard methods of entering data into 'forms' on a computer screen which are designed by the user, and standard simple methods of generating 'reports' which provide output in a suitable user-defined format. There is also, typically, a programming language which permits the package to be prepared so that specific tasks relating to an application are accomplished automatically by selecting the name of a particular program or procedure.

Apart from database packages, other generic software packages include spreadsheets and expert systems shells. These are mainly used in specific applications areas such as accountancy (spreadsheets) and the creation of an expert system (expert systems shells) but in either case the principle is the same: the package can be configured by the user to undertake particular tasks within the capabilities of the package.

If we now compare the advantages and disadvantages of the use of generic software packages against the use of a specialised application, we see that the same issues come into consideration:

- The time involved in configuring a generic package is rather longer than installing a specialised application, but much less than the typical time taken to write programs in conventional high-level language.
- The cost of purchasing a generic applications package is generally less than the cost of a specific application. However, when the cost of configuring the package is added, the saving is likely to be small.
- The generic package is available and can be seen working. Therefore the number of problems in the fully implemented version will be restricted (one hopes) to the errors made in the writing of the specialist routines necessary to configure the package for the application.
- Applications which are implemented by the use of generic applications packages can incorporate more of the original requirements than can those which use a specialised application. This is because there are fewer constraints imposed by a package which is designed to be user-configurable than in one which is designed to be used in its distributed form. Nevertheless, the use of any package inevitably imposes some constraints.

9.5   Conventional high-level language programming

Conventional high-level language programming is considered by many people to be the *natural* way of implementing a software design.

The use of a programming language provides the flexibility to satisfy the requirements exactly as they have been specified without having to make any sacrifices for the sake of the implementation medium. However, the use of high-level programming languages is not cheap, even though the cost of the actual language compiler may be relatively inexpensive. This is because the number of hours work involved in the coding and testing of the required algorithms is considerable. It has been observed that typical complex computer systems take of the order of a person-year to implement in a high-level language. The cost of staff time, and also the cost of having to delay the use of the new system for a substantial period cannot be ignored.

In addition, high-level programming has a history of producing systems which are not bug-free. The testing processes, which we discuss later in this chapter, are by no means foolproof, and there can generally be no absolute guarantee that all possibilities have been checked. In effect, the natural solution, programming in a

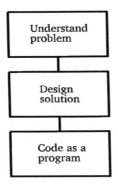

Figure 9.1 Stages in procedural programming

high-level language, has many advantages, but too often the potential hazards are ignored.

Having decided to implement the system using a high-level language, what choice of different high-level languages is there? There are many books available (see, for example, Ford 1990) which discuss a variety of high-level languages and describe the features and strengths and weaknesses of common choices. It should therefore be possible to identify a suitable choice. The choice comes down to the question first of the *type* of programming language under consideration, and second to a choice of the particular programming language for the application.

There are three principal types of programming language:

- Procedural languages
- Declarative languages
- Object-oriented systems.

When people talk about programming languages, they are usually referring to procedural languages, which have for a long time been the most commonly used.

In a procedural language, the programmer describes the algorithms necessary to complete the program. Thus the stages in procedural programming are as shown in Figure 9.1. The programming language will typically give the programmer the opportunity to define the data structures to be used, probably at the beginning of the program, but the task of writing the actual program will centre around the problem of describing in the high-level language each of the algorithms needed.

With a declarative language, we find a completely different approach to the problem. The idea here is that the task of the programmer is to declare to the system, in a clear and unambiguous way, the requirements of the output. No attempt is made to specify how the system should go about finding the necessary output, but instead the program leaves this task to the system (Figure 9.2).

Declarative language programming is a very attractive concept, but the speed of execution of a program in a declarative language is too slow to be accepted for

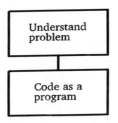

Figure 9.2 Stages in declarative programming

most practical purposes. Thus, the use of declarative languages has a greater part to play today in research than in real practical applications.

Object-oriented programming systems (OOPS) on the other hand, are becoming increasingly widely accepted as a mode for the implementation of computer programs. In OOPS programming, it is possible for the programmer to follow the strategy already identified of making up a program from a set of algorithms and a set of data structures. Object-oriented languages in widespread use are based around a conventional procedural programming language. Within the procedural programming language it is possible to write the algorithms needed for the system. An additional tool is the use of the 'object' which consists of the ability to set up a data item which has associated with it appropriate procedures for its manipulation.

If we think about the definition of an abstract data structure, we know that in order to set up a data structure, we need to describe a way of storing data and a collection of algorithms for the manipulation and maintenance of the data structure. Thus OOPS systems allow us precisely the tools which we need to be able to produce a program which reflects algorithms as procedures within the programs and data structures as objects (Figure 9.3).

9.6 Fourth generation languages (4GLs)

The utopian ideal is to have a computer system which is a fully automated method for generating applications. In an ideal world we would like to have a programming system which asked us a series of questions about what sort of application we wanted and then wrote the programs in an appropriate implementation environment for us! In the real world, it seems unlikely that this ideal situation can be achieved, but nevertheless there have been various attempts to produce systems which go some way towards this.

Fourth generation languages aim to write programs in a painless way after having the requirements described to them. There are some very successful 4GLs which work well for a specific range of applications. Typically, for those areas where there are large numbers of applications which require broadly similar operations and procedures (for example for setting up databases), it has proved relatively

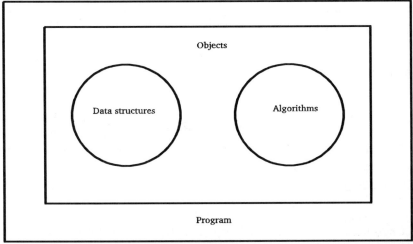

Figure 9.3 OOPS programming

satisfactory to use a 4GL. On the other hand, attempts to provide fully versatile systems which can cope with an unrestricted range of applications have been much less satisfactory.

In terms of the advantages and disadvantages of the use of 4GLs, clearly they can provide a faster solution than the writing of programs in a high-level language, though with less flexibility. Some of the best 4GLs work in similar areas of application to the generic applications software packages described earlier and so a choice needs to be made as to which is more appropriate. In the author's experience, the use of a 4GL for *prototyping* may be justified, and sometimes it may be possible to take the programs developed by the 4GL and use them as a basis for developing the final programs in a high-level language. This can be advantageous, because programs generated by a 4GL are rarely optimised and therefore adjusting them by hand can lead to great improvements in performance.

9.7   To compromise or not to compromise

In most situations, the question of which implementation strategy to adopt is a straightforward choice: Do we choose the fastest, most reliable strategy (some sort of package) at the cost of having to compromise some of the design goals and requirements identified in the definition and specification of the project? Or do we program in high-level language, which will delay the implementation and provide no absolute guarantee that a totally satisfactory program will be the outcome? However, this second approach is almost totally flexible and therefore offers the opportunity to match the definition and specification almost exactly.

From the software engineer's point of view, the most attractive strategy is probably the coding in high-level language of algorithms described in the software design, and for the remainder of this chapter, and much of the next, we shall work on the understanding that this is indeed the strategy adopted. This enables us to cover the material commonly found in books on software engineering. For the moment, therefore, it is appropriate to make some observations about the alternatives:

1. If compromises are made to the design in order to implement in a particular way, then these changes must be recorded and renegotiated with the client. It could be that the changes will change the system little, or that they reflect requirements which should have been included in the original design anyway; or it could be that the package adopted dictates a particular way of doing things inconsistent with the original plan. In any event, it is most important that changes are recorded and agreed.

2. Compromises in design which are made to permit a different sort of implementation will, no doubt, bring benefits too, and these need to be recorded and accounted for. The use of a package which speeds up the development process may, for example, produce a saving in the costs of development or testing, and this should be reflected in the changed agreement with the client.

9.8   Program development in high-level language

Having determined to implement the software using a conventional (procedural) high-level programming language, we shall find that much of the software development method will be prescribed in the software design document which was discussed in Chapter 8. Thus, if the program has been designed in a top-down manner, then the coding is almost certainly best undertaken following the same pattern. Similarly, with programs which have been designed in a bottom-up fashion, the coding may be most appropriately undertaken in the same way.

Many of the issues in writing the code for programs are well known, and it is inappropriate for us to discuss them at length. These include:

1. The use of meaningful variable names and procedure/function names
2. The use of comments in the program to help with subsequent understanding
3. The development of program documentation before programming begins and then the continuous updating of the document if the program changes from its original intentions
4. The use of a team of programmers working on separate modules of the total system.

Other issues are not quite so well known, and we shall spend a little more time on these.

9.8.1 Portability of programs

In order to make the programs written as flexible as possible, it is desirable that they should be *portable*. In other words, we aim to write the programs in such a way that they can easily be adapted to work on hardware combinations different from the one for which they were originally designed.

One factor which influences how possible this will be is the particular programs which are to be written, because some, by their very nature, are designed to operate particular hardware. We sometimes describe such programs as being *architecture dependent*.

For example, software designed for medical use in patient monitoring is likely to be tied very closely to the specialist hardware in use. On the other hand, software designed to run a payroll system should be less restricted to particular choices of printer and disk drives.

A second factor which comes into play is the *selection of the high-level language to be used*. Some languages are notoriously machine dependent, having many different dialects so that programs prepared in the language for a particular machine may need to be almost completely rewritten for an alternative machine. However, other languages are designed to be much more standard which makes software portability a much more realistic possibility (see, for example, Ford 1990).

Another significant factor which restricts program portability is *operating system dependence*. In this case it is the computer's operating system, rather than the particular hardware, which imposes restrictions or offers particular facilities. If these facilities are necessary to the successful completion of the project, then inevitably it will only be possible to port the programs across to other operating systems which provide comparable facilities. Networking or multi-user access to resources are typical facilities which dictate the use of special operating systems.

9.8.2 Reuse of program code

Software engineers often work on projects which require broadly similar techniques and program modules to those which have been used previously, and it is common practice to store those procedures or *program modules* which have already been written and fully tested, so that they can be used in the future, thus saving time and effort. In order to be able to do this, the program modules written are kept as *generic* as possible so that they will be the more easily adapted to future applications.

9.8.3   Use of libraries

Some programming languages go out of their way to encourage the use of proce-dures, functions and other program modules within a new program. Languages such as Modula-2 and C are supported by vast libraries of add-ons which are avail-able to software engineers. The task of writing many programs can be reduced to finding and configuring commercial modules to the requirements of the current project, then writing the necessary program segments to join them together.

Naturally, the purchase of these ready-made program sections is expensive, but it has advantages of saving time in the software development process and of guar-anteeing the quality and testing of the software. Program modules which have been commercially marketed form a very important part of the software engineer's toolkit.

9.9   Formal approaches to implementation

When we discussed the software specification process, we identified the use of formal methods as being an appropriate way of specifying our requirements for a particular project in a clear and unambiguous way. These methods, based on some simple mathematical processes, provide a medium for the description of algorithms (see Appendix I and Ford and Ford 1993).

The formal description of the algorithms is *implicit,* in that it does not state *how* the software is to be written, but instead concentrates on a description of what exactly the software must do. Therefore programs specified in this way need to be *realised* in an actual implementation.

The theory behind the use of the formal methods is that it should be possible to convert the implicit and mathematical specification in a series of stages, each of which makes some progress towards an explicit program. At each of these stages, it should be possible to see that the current stage is exactly equivalent to the previous one, and therefore the room for error is eliminated.

In practice, the use of formal methods to specify and implement non-trivial software problems in this sort of way is complex and it is not widely used outside of research establishments. It is nevertheless important, as we shall see when we are discussing testing of software, to recognise this alternative mode of development (see also Appendix I).

9.10   The role of software tools in implementation

We have described already the various stages which software tools, such as CASE workbenches, can assist and inform in the software development process, and at the stage of the program design, we were able to identify how the various parts of

```
function mean1:integer;
var i:integer;
    begin
    for i := 1 to 20 do
        begin
        writeln('type in a number');
        readln(number[i])
        end;
    total := 0;
    for i := 1 to 20 do
        total := total + number[i];
    mean1 := total/20
    end;



function mean2:integer;
var i:integer;
    begin
    total := 0;
    for i := 1 to 20 do
        begin
        writeln('type in a number');
        readln(number);
        total := total + number;
        end;
    mean2 := total/20
    end;
```

Figure 9.4 In the second version of this procedure, unnecessary repetition is eliminated, which speeds up execution

the project were stored in the data dictionary, and reflected in the diagrammatic representations. We were also able to produce reports of the software design.

For many users of CASE tools, the tool has no further role to play, but some tools do offer the facility to generate program code in a particular high-level language. Thus, the work of putting the information relating to the project into the CASE tool is rewarded, not merely by the improved error and consistency checking which the tool can undertake, but also by the production of the final program.

As in our discussion of 4GLs, CASE-generated code has various shortcomings. It is often restricted to particular programming languages, and to particular styles of problem. It is also considered by many people that the code produced is of more value as a prototype of the solution than as the final product. This is because the programs are rarely optimised by the tools. The tools adopt a naive approach which may involve needless repetition, which a programmer, with insight, can remove (see Figure 9.4 for an example of optimisation of code).

The use of CASE tools to generate program code is nevertheless an area likely to expand in importance in future.

9.11   Exercises

Selt-test questions

1. Would a specialist package or a generic package provide more flexibility to adapt to changing circumstances?
2. Identify three applications where it is desirable for software to be portable and three where portability is less important.
3. Which is better: a program which is based around standard libraries of procedures and functions, or one which is specially written in its entirety?

Exercises

1. Find an organisation which has adopted a packaged software solution. What advantages and disadvantages have they discovered?
2. For each of the following applications, determine which modes of implementation would be worthy of further consideration:

    (a) A small company payroll

    (b) Simple company accounts

    (c) A warehouse stock-control system

    (d) Inland Revenue tax records

    (e) A local lottery.

3. Write a skeleton program which reads data from a file and prints out selected records. Use memorable variable and procedure names. When the program is complete, show it to a friend and ask for an explanation of what the program does. If your choices of names are good, then the program should be easy to follow.

Chapter 10

Programming techniques

10.1 Introduction

In this chapter we discuss the variety of programming techniques and methods which may be employed. Chapter 9 described how a suitable implementation *medium* would be chosen to suit the project in question. Here we assume that a conventional programming solution has been selected, and the discussion is based upon traditional programming methods and modern approaches to them.

10.2 Making a start

By this stage in the computer software development project, we have a complete program design available (see Chapter 8) and we have decided upon the implementation medium, which we have assumed to be the use of some high-level language. As we discussed in Chapter 9, it will be important that the language selected gives us the facilities and tools for the project.

The first task of the programmer is to become familiar with the language and the way in which it is used. Normally, it is assumed that a language is chosen with which the programmer team is familiar, but this cannot always be the case. New languages appear, which offer new facilities needed in a project, or a particular organisation may standardise all applications development on a particular language not widely used.

Gaining familiarity with a programming language means more than simply learning the syntax of the language instructions. It is important that the programmers also study the *philosophy* of the language, so they may appreciate *how* it should be used. For example, some computer languages are designed to make it particularly easy to develop programs using *dynamic data structures* or *procedures*. Other languages would encourage an approach based upon *static data structures* and *functions*. For many applications, it would not really matter whether the data structures used were dynamic or static. Nor would it matter whether the program structure is imposed through the use of procedures or functions. It is far more important for the programmer to ensure that the work done uses the features which the language is designed to provide, rather than using all possible ingenuity to produce a program which is really more suitable to a different language.

10.3   Choosing an implementation strategy

The actual approach to implementation is likely to be closely governed by the form of the program design presented to the programmer team. Here we identify three possible ways in which the program design may appear, each based upon a different approach to the program specification.

10.3.1   Formal description

It may be that the program specification has been written using a formal method. In this case, a formal description in the formal language will exist for each of the program procedures. It will have been the task of the software engineers at the design stage to indicate *how* the various procedures within the system are to be *interlinked*, but the clear and unambiguous descriptions of the program statements will appear in the formal description language.

   The task for the programming team will therefore be to code the formal descriptions in the programming language chosen for the implementation. As we have discussed previously, it should be possible, in theory at least, for the programmers to complete a formal *proof* that the programs designed and specified using the formal method are *precisely equivalent* to the ones developed in the high-level programming language (see Appendix I).

10.3.2   Pseudocode

As an alternative to specifications based upon a formal method, we saw that descriptions could be based upon a high-level programming language such as ADA or Pascal. In this case, we may describe the program design as being in *pseudocode,* since each part of the design is described in an approximation to the programming language in question.

   The task for the programmer is to convert the pseudocode descriptions into programs written in the selected high-level language. It will be most satisfactory to do this when the programs are to be written in the language which forms the basis for the pseudocode. Sometimes this may not be the case, and in this event the programmers need to take particular care.

For the reasons described above, it could be that the implementational medium adopts different strategies for the implementation of particular features of a program design, and that the pseudodescription adopts different approaches again. It is particularly awkward for the programmer if two opposing strategies have to be reconciled at each point in the program implementation.

Fortunately, in most cases, the pseudocode description can be provided in a way which is fairly implementation free. This can be done either by using very general descriptions of what is to happen, or by ensuring that such widely available specific techniques are described, for example loops, arrays, etc., that they may be implemented in any normal computer language.

10.3.3 Diagrammatic approaches

The design may be communicated in the form of a diagram or diagrams. We have used the Jackson's structure diagram elsewhere in this book, because we consider it to be a very appropriate diagrammatic representation of the program design. However, other diagrams may be used equally well. Starting from a diagrammatic specification, the programmer has much more freedom to work on developing the program code, because the diagrams are less prescriptive in describing *precisely* what must be done. On the other hand, this is not necessarily an advantage, since it implies that the diagrams admit a greater degree of ambiguity in the definitions of requirements and design, and therefore this may make quality control more difficult.

10.3.4 Hybrid approaches

In practice, hybrid approaches to program design, based upon more than one of the above methods, are very likely to be found. Diagrammatic representations give a very good overall view of the different procedures to be developed, and how they should interrelate. However, as we saw, diagrams are less good at describing the requirements fully and unambiguously. Therefore a more definite and detailed design for the individual components of the system, based on pseudocode descriptions or formal specifications may accompany the diagrams.

10.4   Working through the method

The processes involved in the implementation of the programs, that is, the actual writing of the code in a suitable computer language, are dependent upon the thoroughness of the previous (design) stage. In theory, at least, all the important issues are dealt with during design, and all the decisions taken simply need to be put into practice during implementation. This has led to the view, held by some in the computer industry, that the actual programming task requires little skill or insight, since it is mainly concerned with copying and translating without the need for creativity. This is not a view which we would support, but it is one which must be recognised.

For this reason, it becomes difficult to be certain who will be involved in writing the program code. In the best practice, software engineers who designed the system or who have been a part of the team working on the system will be employed. In other cases specialist programmers will be used. These are people who do not have the experience or training in design and specification methods, but concentrate instead upon the writing of accurate and efficient computer programs. In either case, we shall refer to the people involved in writing the programs as *programmers.*

The main task of the programmer is to work on converting the algorithms described in the program design into statements in the appropriate high-level language. Naturally, there is the need to work efficiently and accurately, and to take careful note of any seeming inconsistencies in the design which become apparent during the programming because it is only at this stage that certain inconsistencies in the specification and design stages may come to light, even though they should have been detected earlier. High-quality software development relies upon the programmer being fully aware of the intentions of the software specification and design, and checking that the software fulfills those intentions and following the design rigidly.

Additionally, the programmer may notice that additional functionality could be built in easily at the implementation stage, even though it was not requested in the design and specification. This will usually be a result of the particular method of implementation or of the language selected, which may offer unexpectedly helpful opportunities for development. A programmer who notices these possibilities can draw them to the attention of the designers.

The stages which we can identify in good programming practice are:

- Understand the objectives of the software development
- Understand the design document
- Determine a strategy for program development
- Agree a project plan
- Write the program code
- Check the programs for accuracy
- Complete the programmer-written documentation
- Be involved in the introduction of the programs with users and user training.

As with several other areas within this book, we cannot be prescriptive, either in the order in which activities need to be done, nor in the precise list of activities. However, it is true to say that many software development projects suffer from too narrow a view of the role of the programmer.

```
┌─────────────────────────────────┐
│                                 │
│   Patient makes appointment     │
│                                 │
└─────────────────────────────────┘
```

Figure 10.1 Single-block diagram for dental appointment system

10.5 A strategy for program development

Part of the *strategy for program development* is implicit when the programming team is selected. Is it a team of specialist programmers who play little part in the design processes, or will the software engineers themselves be involved in writing the programs? There are other issues involved too, some of which relate directly to the design methods adopted.

The two principal methods of program implementation are based around top-down design and bottom-up design. The strategies for writing the code are described in the same way.

10.5.1 Top-down or bottom-up programming?

In **top-down programming**, the whole problem to be solved has been subdivided into a series of smaller problems (Figure 10.1). Each of these smaller problems is successively subdivided (Figures 10.2 and 10.3).

The programming processes are undertaken in a similar way. The programmers begin by writing a program which shows how the main components of the system interrelate. Each of these major components is then written with successive levels of refinement being introduced as the programmer proceeds to greater levels of detail. We shall meet this idea again later in the chapter. Figures representing the stages of program development are given in Section 10.8.

As can be seen from the diagrams, in order to write programs at the highest levels which can be run, *dummy* procedures have been written to correspond to the procedures required at the next level down. These dummy procedures are

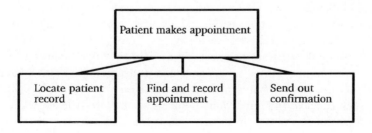

Figure 10.2 More detailed structure diagram for dental appointment system

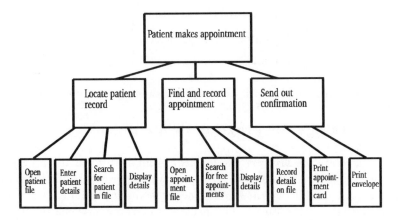

Figure 10.3 Detailed structure diagram of dental appointment system

known as *stubs* and play a fundamental part in the testing of computer software which has been developed in a top-down way.

One possible problem with top-down programming is that it adopts the approach that the detail of the problem may be left quite safely until later, so particular difficulties in implementing the lower levels will not be discovered until that point is reached, by which time other decisions may have been made which make it difficult to alter the implementation to solve the problems. For this reason, bottom-up programming may be preferred.

In **bottom-up programming**, the opposite approach is taken. The development process begins at the bottom level of the structure diagram by tackling the most detailed level and developing procedures. These procedures are then progressively joined together to make successive higher levels in the diagram.

The advantage of bottom-up program development is that any particular problems of implementation in the detail of the requirements can be tackled first. This avoids any possibility that the higher levels will need to be redesigned later to cope with a problem in the implementation at a lower level. However, the problem with bottom-up development is that it is rather common for the different procedures at the lowest levels to adopt different approaches to solving particular problems within the implementation. It therefore becomes less likely that pieces of program code can be reused within the system and also may increase the likelihood of both errors in the code, and of slower execution.

In practice, many software engineers appreciate that both methods of development have their important features, and that it is desirable to reach a compromise, within which the best features of both methods can be realised. These *hybrid* methods seek to solve the important problems at the lowest level, while retaining the advantages of the top-down design. Most practical software development will adopt some hybrid approach, even though it is often referred to as being *top-down*.

10.6 Agree a project plan

The software development industry is well known for its historical failure to deliver to deadlines in more than a few projects. There are several reasons for this. They include the rapid pace of hardware developments, which can mean that the goalposts are moved several times within the period of development. There is also the difficulty, which we have identified elsewhere, of the intangible nature of the product, and the consequent difficulty of getting the specification right first time. Nevertheless the development of a project plan is important and is a key to ensuring the delivery of an appropriate system.

The *strategy* adopted provides the basis of the formulation of the project plan. Assuming that a hybrid approach to development is adopted, it will be critical to decide which elements of the lowest level in the design should most appropriately be developed first, and which elements should be left for development later. The use of a team in the development also implies the need for a strategy which describes how the various members of the team will work together. For example, will different team members be wholly responsible for developing different parts of the system, or will a chief programmer allocate particular tasks, according to who becomes available at particular stages? Alternatively, will tasks be allocated according to the *nature* of a particular part of the problem, so that the programmer best suited to this part of the development is chosen?

The organisation of the team is also important. Are members of the team under the control of a chief programmer, which makes management of the team straightforward, but does not necessarily lead to optimal performance by individual members of the team? Alternatively, the team may have joint responsibility for the project, which means that a team spirit may develop. On the other hand, in the worst circumstances, corporate responsibility can mean that nobody is responsible, which can lead to disastrous results.

Software quality control is an important issue in any software engineering project, and the strategy for quality assurance needs to be built into the project plan. Some methods of quality assurance may need to be a part of the programming work from the beginning. Other methods take a more detached standpoint and rely on testing the completed system at the end of the development. Both the methods and the time allocation for testing and correction of errors should be included in the plan for the programming.

When the project plan is agreed, a project chart is usually drawn up. This can take the form of Figure 10.4.

10.7 Write the program code

If all the preliminary investigations and specification and design, and the project plans have been constructed thoroughly, the programming itself should be routine.

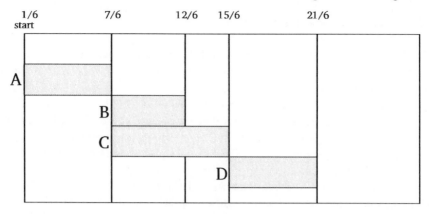

Figure 10.4 Bar chart

The chosen language should provide the facilities for the conversion of the require-ments into the actual lines of program code in a routine way. In this section we identify several important issues:

- Reuse of program code
- Use of library routines
- Portability of programs
- Consultation with other team members
- Changing the specifications and design.

The reuse of program code can be a very important device in increasing the speed and accuracy of programming. If a simple procedure is designed to be used in several places within a programming project, then the cost and time savings in writing it once and then reusing it elsewhere can be considerable. In addition, once a particular program segment has been checked for errors, and found to be error free, then the reoccurences of it are guaranteed error free. Similarly, if errors should arise later, they will only need to be corrected in the single procedure, rather than separately and independently at all places in the program.

A similar approach can be based on the adoption of library procedures. Many software developers keep a record of the standard procedures and functions which they have written and fully tested in other projects. It can then be very quick and cost effective to introduce previously developed code within the present project. A variation of this approach is also possible in languages where prewritten library procedures are marketed commercially. Here they can be purchased and incorpo-rated in the program being developed.

There can be two costs arising from the use of library procedures. One is that the library procedures themselves can be expensive. This cost tends to be small when compared with the cost of program development and testing. More worryingly is the tendency among some programmers to prefer to use library procedures wherever possible and to try to adapt software designs to fit into commercially available procedures. These changes in design can occasionally be justified if the programs can be completed sooner at less cost and with greater confidence of quality, but only if they have been fully investigated at all levels of the software engineering process and incorporated into amended versions of the specification and design as appropriate.

Programs developed need to be as portable as possible, and in certain cases the requirement for portability is built into the specification explicitly as a feature. Modern high-level languages can provide good facilities for the development of portable programs, because they usually conform rigidly to an agreed and well-understood standard. Therefore provided that the programmers do not break the rules of the language to gain advantages from hardware-specific oppportunities (such as writing directly to screen memory to increase the speed of the display) there should be few problems with developing portable programs. This desire should, however, be considered when specifying the implementational language, since choice of language is the single most significant influence on the portability of the result.

The importance in any team programming project of continuous consultation with other team members to discuss difficulties in implementation and the resulting minor changes in design is most important. Far too often, one of the problems in the quality of the completed program is that the program sections do not fit together properly. This can be the result of individualist programmers writing parts of the program in their own way, rather than adhering strictly to the specification.

There are really two issues at stake here. The first should come under the heading of project management, since it refers to the question of how the programmers are to be organised and managed. Is there, for example, a chief programmer who controls and directs the work of the team? In this case, consultation will need to be between individual members of the team and the chief programmer who will then make the decision as to how the work should proceed. Where a chief programmer is in control, the line of authority is clear: the chief programmer's decision is final. However, the chief programmer model of management is not universally adopted. One reason for this is that programmers do not always work best when under the direction of a leader, and many organisations prefer to adopt a structure where team work is built up through the use of a peer group of programmers with joint responsibility. Decisions need to be taken by consensus, and agreement with all members of the team is necessary before changes can be introduced (Figure 10.5).

Each strategy has its advantages and disadvantages. The team model has the advantage that individuals often work well with their peers within a team, but the disadvantage that there is nobody in overall control who can make a final decision. On the other hand, all members of the team are kept informed of all changes in the design, and not just those which directly affect them, which has added quality control value. With a chief programmer structure, it is essential that the chief programmer gets on well with the other members of the team, and that they respect him or her. Resentment of the manager of any organisation is a common problem and this can easily develop if individual members of the programming

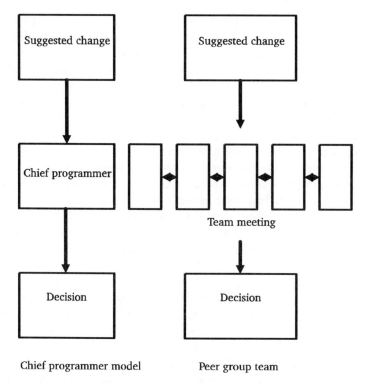

Chief programmer model   Peer group team

Figure 10.5 Different programming team management affects the decision making process

team feel that their ideas are being stifled by an unsympathetic chief programmer.

The second issue relates to the control of maverick programmers while encouraging creativity. This is particularly difficult within any joint software development process. The root of the problem is that most programmers develop their own techniques for writing programs. These techniques and the approach adopted may not mesh well with the approaches of other team members. This means that, to develop a neat final outcome, some members of the team may need to be forced to work in a way they would not have chosen. This naturally can cause ill-feeling, and the programs may be less satisfactory if the team members feel that they are being forced to work below their standard.

Two things can help. First, after a team has been working together for some time, it may become apparent that particular team members have ability in developing specific types of code. This in itself can be a great help, because if each member concentrates on developing the types of program module which are most suited to the programmer's ability then both the quality, the speed of production and the motivation of the team member are likely to improve. Second, it can be useful for individual members of a team to share their different ideas about how parts of the program should be implemented. This can be a very useful staff development exercise for the team members, since it allows them to evaluate critically different ways of approaching problems and to identify which are most appropriate for the present project.

In any project, it is likely to become apparent at some stage that it is necessary to change the specification and design. This may be because consultation with some of the users indicates that there was an error at the analysis and design stage, or because the programmers discover some problem, either with the implementation environment or with the hardware. Of course, none of these situations should arise in theory, since the quality controls built in at every stage should have removed any possible ambiguity or doubt. In practical software development, however, changes do become necessary.

The programming team may decide to:

1. Pretend the problem is not there and develop the system as originally planned
2. Solve the problem without disclosing that it arose
3. Enter into a full discussion of the problem and the changes needed with clients and software engineers at every level.

There are no prizes for guessing which of these three options is the one favoured by the authors, but it is instructive to consider for a moment why the first two options may seem attractive to the programming team.

Software engineering is all about improving the quality of the software development process, and the emphasis is on getting the requirements, the specification, the design and the implementation as problem free as possible. There may therefore be a belief that to admit a problem at any of the earlier stages when it comes to the software implementation is to admit that the quality controls have failed. Of course this is not really the case, since it is precisely the fact that the problem can be noticed at this late stage which adds to the quality control mechanisms within the development process. The crucial thing is for the client to understand that an admission that things have gone wrong with the initial design and that changes need to be discussed is a sign of strength rather than of weakness.

Of course, it is human nature to be reluctant to admit failures which might be the responsibility of the software engineering team, but quality control demands that these disclosures be made.

10.8 Check the programs for accuracy

Earlier in this chapter, we considered two fundamental approaches to design: *top-down design* and *bottom-up design* and we suggested that of the two a top-down approach was often to be favoured. We also identified that a hybrid approach which capitalises on the strengths of both top-down and bottom-up methods can be best of all. Earlier in this chapter we considered approaches to the actual writing

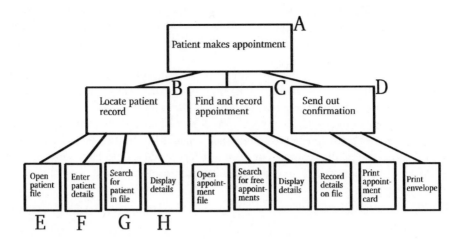

Figure 10.6 Detailed structure diagram of dental appointment system

of programs and again we met the distinction between top-down and bottom-up approaches.

Not to be confused with these methods of software design and of program writing are two approaches to software **testing**:

1. Top-down program testing
2. Bottom-up program testing.

Paradoxically, perhaps, the bottom-up approach to program testing is the one we favour.

10.8.1   Top-down testing

In top-down testing, we can imagine a program which is under development. The program has an overall structure which is represented in Figure 10.6. For convenience, we are adopting the same overall structure as represented in Figures 10.1-10.3. The figure is a Jackson's structure diagram which represents the interrelationship of the procedures and program modules, which, for convenience, we have labelled *A, B, C, etc.*.

To implement this program, we would probably begin from the top of the structure diagram by writing a routine undertaken first, which calls the processes from the first level down of the structure diagram. The first procedure to be written is variously described as the function *main()* in a C-language program, as the main body of a Pascal program or as the *main driving program.*

Using structured English, we may write an appropriate representation of this first procedure (Figure 10.7).

Procedure: patient makes appointment
```
Locate patient record
Find and record appointment
Send out confirmation
```

Figure 10.7 Structured English representation of the procedure in box A of Figure 10.9

A top-down testing method dictates that we should now test this subprogram before we go on to write any further parts of the program. But clearly this will be difficult, since parts of the program called by this main process are not yet available, so an error will be reported.

The solution to this problem, as we saw earlier, is to write a *dummy procedure* for each of the processes listed in the main process. Again, using structured English, a typical representation of a dummy procedure, or *stub* for process A is shown in Figure 10.8.

So, having replaced all the procedures in the first level of the structure diagram by stubs, it is now possible to test the main procedure. Once any problems with it have been eliminated, each stub is changed progressively into its realisation. Thus, referring to Figure 10.6, we can observe that process A will be realised by the creation of three new stubs, also shown in Figure 10.8.

At each stage in the process, one procedure is realised and then the resulting program is tested. The theory is that eventually an error will be identified, and it should occur in the procedure which was last converted from a stub to its realisation. In practice, since the testing process is never quite as thorough as it should be, the error might occur elsewhere, and this is something of a weakness in the top-down approach to testing.

Other criticisms of the top-down approach include the observation that writing so many stubs is tedious.

10.8.2   Bottom-up testing

With bottom-up testing, the idea is that, having developed each of the procedures represented in a structure diagram for the program, each is tested independently, and then the procedures are built up into subprocesses. Each subprocess is then tested, and when the testing is complete, these are joined to form the entire program, which is then tested as a whole. This process is represented in Figures 10.9-10.11.

The disadvantage of bottom-up testing is that to test each procedure, we shall need to write a specific program which will give the procedure the inputs it requires and which will display the outputs of the procedure for verification.

In terms of the program represented in Figure 10.11, we shall therefore need to write the following special test programs:

```
procedure MakeAppointment;
     begin
     LocatePatientRec;
     FindAppointment;
     ConfirmAppointment;
     end;
```

Stub for the process in box A of Figure 10.6

```
procedure LocatePatientRec;
     begin
     OpenPatfile;
     EnterPatDetails;
     FindPat;
     DisplayPat;
     end;
```

Stub for procedure in box B of Figure 10.6

```
procedure OpenPatFile;
     begin
     writeln('procedure OpenPatFile');
     end;
```

Stub for procedure in box E of Figure 10.6

Figure 10.8   Top-down testing may be carried out by producing dummy procedures

Figure 10.9 Lowest level procedures are tested in isolation

- Eight programs to test the bottom level of procedures
- Three programs to test the middle level of procedures.

In order to indicate what is involved in writing the test programs, the process is illustrated in Figure 10.12.

The main advantage of bottom-up testing over top-down testing is that the errors are more likely to be identified and placed within a confined part of the program, rather than with top-down testing where at the end, errors which arise at the bottom level could be as a result of errors in almost any of the most detailed level of procedures.

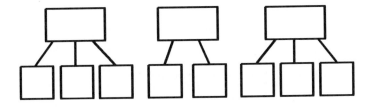

Figure 10.10 Lowest level procedures are integrated and tested at the next level up

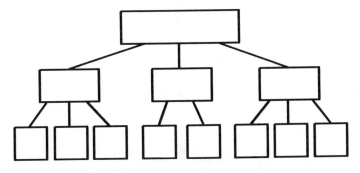

Figure 10.11 The entire program is tested at the highest level

10.8.3 Alpha and beta testing

The testing processes described so far are those undertaken as the software is changed from a design into a reality. But eventually the software is complete and needs to be tested before it is released live. This final testing is often performed in two stages.

In alpha testing of software the whole package is tested carefully and thoroughly by a team of programmers to simulate the software's performance in real use. The idea is that alpha testing should allow for any remaining problems to be highlighted and ironed out before any real users try the software.

Beta testing happens after alpha testing is complete. In beta testing, a number of typical users of the system are identified and invited to try out a prerelease (beta test) version of the software. They use the software as if it was the final-released version and report any errors and problems encountered. Beta test sites usually receive their software at discount prices.

10.8.4 But how should the software be tested?

Most software performs well when undertaking standard applications, and problems frequently arise when the software is subjected to unexpected combinations.

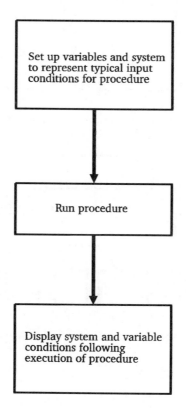

Figure 10.12 Stages involved in testing a procedure

It is therefore necessary that software should be tested:

- To check all normal pathways through the programs
- To check all predicted error conditions through the software
- To check as many as possible of the unpredictable and failure situations as can be imagined.

One way of undertaking the tests is a method known as *equivalence partitioning*. In this method, data which have common characteristics and which should therefore be treated in the same way are identified as being equivalent, and at least one item of data out of each of the different *equivalence classes* is selected for the test.

So, for example, a program which follows one rule for women over 60 and another for women 60 or under would have two women aged 30 and 40 in the same equivalence class, since both should be dealt with identically. There should be no need to test with a women aged 30 and again with a woman aged 40, provided that the program has reproduced the conditions faithfully.

Unfortunately, programs do not always meet their specifications. As a result, this naive approach to testing is hardly adequate. For example, the programmer might have mistakenly fixed the border between older and younger women at 35, simply by a typing mistake. In this case, the program would test accurately for a woman of 30, and accurately for a woman of 65, but for reasons not obvious from the original specification, it would behave wrongly with a woman of 40.

All of this shows that testing programs based simply upon their original specification is dangerous. It is far more sensible to examine the code and identify critical values where a decision is to be taken. It should then be possible to predict from the specification how values should be treated on each side of the critical value and test these values accordingly.

In the case we have just discussed, a glance at the program code would identify the age 35 as critical for the program, and would prompt tests for women of 34, 35 and 36; while a glance at the specification without looking at the program would have identified 59, 60 and 61 as the appropriate values.

We distinguish between testing methods based upon looking at the specification and not the program (i.e. treating the program as a black box) as *black box testing* while testing based upon examination of the program code is *white box testing*.

So, programs need to be tested thoroughly, and to avoid tests which reproduce the programmers' own prejudices as to the selection of data for testing, it is appropriate for the final alpha tests to be undertaken using data selected independently. The selected test data for a program are sometimes known as a *test suite* and are probably most appropriately chosen by the systems analysts responsible for the original definition of the problem.

10.9   The fundamental problem with program testing

The biggest problem with program testing is that, however many tests are carried out, they can never exhaust the possibilities. Tests are very good at showing up errors in logic which affect the whole program, but many bugs actually exist because of some simple error, such as the typing of 35 instead of 60, in the example above. It is therefore appropriate to consider whether there are alternatives to testing readily available, and to consider the overheads of these alternatives.

10.10   Alternatives to testing

We have identified two realistic alternatives to testing. For those who use formal methods for the specification and realisation of the software, testing can be replaced by the formal proof of satisfaction which the realisation is of the specification. Readers interested in this should refer to Appendix I, or to Ford and Ford (1993).

Alternatively, static program analysis consists of examining the code in some detail. Various techniques are described (for example, in Sommerville (1989)). We may observe that one method based upon this approach consists of examining the program code and writing a careful specification of what it does. This can then be compared with the original specification of the problem and any differences can be identified.

10.11   Complete the programmer-written documentation

Documentation of the entire software development project is important to ensure that there is a clear statement of the objectives and the design of the system. However, the documentation which becomes central to the maintenance of the programs is that prepared by the programmer.

It is important to remember that the program documentation forms a part of this larger document, because it helps to focus on its role. The programmer has taken the design which has already been completed, based upon the specifications and produced the programs which implement the design. Therefore the key elements of the programmer's documentation are:

- The names of the procedures written
- How the procedures interrelate
- Any particular methods and approaches applied within the implementation which were not specified in the design
- The rationale for any changes to the design which were incorporated at the programming stage
- Full details of the testing undertaken, confirmation that quality has been assured and descriptions of any remaining bugs or weaknesses in the programs.

One common difficulty with the documentation produced by programmers is that many engaged in writing computer programs find the programming itself enjoyable and the writing of documentation is therefore the least interesting part of the work. For this reason it may be neglected or completed quickly with insufficient thought. Software engineers may be more interested in producing documentation than programmers, or they may employ a documentation specialist within the software engineering team. This specialist in technical writing can also be engaged in the writing of the user guide.

10.12   Be involved in the introduction of the programs with users and user training

We have described already the use of beta tests to assure the quality of the programs being written. This involves the software engineers in preparing a version of the programs for use by a test site. These software engineers will then provide training for the users on site and monitor closely the performance of the system.

The opportunity for beta testing also gives the software engineers a chance to understand which aspects of the system's use give particular difficulties to the users. For example, it could be that the day-to-day entry of data and checking and processing of orders in a stock control system are very easy and straightforward to operate. On the other hand, it may be that addition of stock to the system when there is a delivery from a supplier requires particular care.

This could be for a number of reasons. One possible motive might have been the desire to make the day-to-day running of the system as straightforward as possible, and therefore a disproportionate amount of effort might have been employed to ensure user-friendliness. The addition of stock to the system could have been considered as a more specialist task and therefore less time will have been spent on its design.

The information gained from seeing users operating the system helps the software engineers to refine the user guide, and to design training courses for the users. User training and documentation must be prepared for different audiences if the system is complex. It could be, for example, that the people in charge of the system need to know how to undertake more unusual and complex tasks, but that the majority of operators only really need to know about the common tasks. This would imply two versions of the user guide and two types of training programme.

10.13 Data types, data structures and data reification

One feature of software design identified is the need to develop suitable data structures for the storage and manipulation of the data held by the system. Naturally, it is within the programming phase in the system's development that data structures actually come into existence, and therefore we consider here some of the aspects of this.

The data dictionary contains details of all the data structures for the system. Schneider and Bruell (1991) list the characteristics which are included:

1. Data structure name
2. General description of that data structure (e.g. linear, hierarchical, random access, direct access, internal, external)
3. Information fields contained within the data structure
4. Operations that can be performed on the data structure. For each operation we describe the state of the data structure before and after the operation
5. What other modules access this structure; what other modules modify this structure
6. Limitations or restrictions placed on this data structure.

The programmer's task is then to develop a suitable realisation or implementation of the data structure. In other words, we need to develop a suitable method for storing and manipulating the data.

To help understand the concept of a data structure from a programmer's viewpoint, we may consider it as being:

- A way of storing data in a particular form
- A series of procedures for the manipulation of the data stored in the form described.

The term *data reification* describes the relationship between the data structure, which is defined in abstract terms in the software specification, and its implementation using actual computer programming statements (see, for example, Ford and Ford 1993).

10.14   Optimisation

For many years, optimisation of computer programs has been an important issue. It refers to the concept of making the programs as *efficient* as possible. However, the difficulty arises as to how one might measure efficiency!

Traditionally programs have been optimised against one of two criteria. Some programs have been developed to optimise computer memory usage, by being as compact as possible, while other programs have been developed to be optimal from an execution speed viewpoint, to be as fast as possible.

Unfortunately, it tends to be impossible to optimise programs for both of these criteria, as the more rapid the code developed, often the more long-winded the program needs to be. In addition, there are other possible candidates for optimisation. We have identified the following list:

1. Speed of execution
2. Size
3. Reliability
4. Speed of programming
5. Ease of programming
6. User-friendliness
7. Portability
8. Maintainability.

Each of these aspirations is clearly desirable in most programs. Unfortunately, it is usually impossible to optimise for any single quality without compromising the program with respect to a rival.

The optimisation of programs to give the fastest possible execution speed has been singled out as being particularly important. *Benchmarking* describes the process where rival implementations of a particular specification compete over timed trials to determine which operates the fastest.

10.15   Programming tools

We discussed in Chapter 5 the use of various software tools in the software engineering process. Programmers have for many years applied tools to assist in their work, without many really realising their range or significance. In this section we shall identify a range of tools frequently used:

1. The editor. This is the tool which allows the entry of the program code. Good editors help the programmer to make changes, to move code around and to set the program out attractively and correctly.
2. Comparison tools. These tools allow the programmer to compare two files for differences. One common problem in programming is that in an attempt to copy sections of code from one place to another, something becomes corrupted or lost. Therefore the ability to check for errors in two copies of the same code is a great advantage.
3. Debuggers can allow a programmer to run through a program which is under development one step at a time. Therefore it becomes possible to check exactly where an error arises in a program. Debuggers can also often give information about the values of variables when a problem has arisen.
4. Tracers operate by giving details of where a program has reached in execution at different stages. This provides the same sort of information as is provided by a debugger to help locate program errors.
5. Static program analysers are not very common, but examine the code written to establish whether or not it is consistent with the design specification. This is accomplished in various ways, typically by investigating the outcomes of decisions taken within the program.
6. Compilers and interpreters are the programmer's key tools. How efficient they are at drawing attention to inconsistencies and errors, and at locating bugs at the correct place in the programmer's code determines to a great extent how efficiently programs can be developed and debugged.

10.16   Exercises

1. Write out a version of the program from Figure 10.9 in a language of your choice. Show how each stub is changed into the realisation of the procedure.
2. Show how the programs described here would be implemented in your favourite programming language.
3. (For discussion) See how many additional qualities you can add to the list for possible optimisation.
4. For a dentist's reception system, place in order of importance, the qualities you have listed.
5. To what extent would you need to change your list and your priorities for:

- A cardiac monitoring unit?
- A guided missile control system?
- A warehouse stock control system?

Chapter 11

Software maintenance

11.1 Introduction

In this chapter, we describe the issues involved in software maintenance. Maintenance of computer software is a complex issue, both because of the complicated nature of the problem and because of the enormous sums of money spent each year on software maintenance. Here we identify why software needs to be maintained, how it should be maintained, and ways of keeping the cost of software maintenance as low as possible.

11.2 Software maintenance: the costs

Estimates of the annual cost of maintaining computer software already written vary widely, but range between 50 and 80% of the total software development budget in any given period. In other words, for every pound spent on developing software, it is claimed that at least a further pound will be spent on software maintenance during the life of the program.

Clearly, with the costs of software maintenance being at least as great as the costs of initial software development, there needs to be some detailed consideration of methods which can lead to reducing these costs. We shall see in this chapter how some of the costs of software maintenance will be reduced naturally as a result of the introduction of the software engineering methods discussed elsewhere in this book.

11.3   What is software maintenance?

If we talk about motor car maintenance, then we have a clear understanding of
exactly what that particular term means. Cars need to be serviced *routinely* to
check whether parts are wearing out gradually, and to renew the oil, filters and
brakes. In addition, cars have to be maintained to repair components which fail
suddenly in use.

Software maintenance is different. Pieces of a computer program do not simply
wear out, because they have been used too often. Nor does a procedure which
worked perfectly well yesterday suddenly fail catastrophically so that it will no
longer work at all. Instead, we meet a different range of causes which mean that
software needs to be changed or repaired:

- The software may contain bugs which have been known about and need to
  be corrected at the earliest opportunity. Sometimes these bugs appear at the
  last testing of the software before release. They may be tolerated as being
  insufficiently serious to stop release of the software. But after the correction
  of the bugs a *patched* version of the program will be released.
- The software may contain bugs which come to light because of changing
  demands made upon it by users. Often software contains bugs within little-
  used sections of the programs which only come to light some considerable
  time after the software is introduced.
- Changing requirements of the user may mean that the software specification
  is no longer up to the users' new requirements. In this case, the software
  can hardly be described as having bugs, since it performs faithfully to its
  specification. Nevertheless, changes in the software are necessary to fit the
  users' changed requirements.
- Changing hardware platforms may mean that software which performed perfectly well on the previous generation of hardware now performs inadequately.
  This is particularly common in the need to provide output in a form suitable
  for a constantly changing range of printers.

All of this means that software maintenance should be seen as a *natural* part
of software use, in exactly the same way that motor car maintenance is seen as a
natural part of car ownership. However, there is one critical difference, which makes
software maintenance that much more important. The car owner who cannot find
anybody to maintain a particular car to the required standard has the choice of
swapping the car for a different model. It may be an expensive option but, once
a new car is purchased, the problems of the poorly maintained previous model
disappear at a stroke.

The software owner who can find no way of maintaining a software package to
the required standard faces a much more serious dilemma. Typically a software
system adopted by a company will contain a lot of critical data and records which
the company must retain. The data may be crucial to the company's sales and

marketing, or to its supply chain. Whatever happens, the data must remain accessible. But swapping to a different software system takes time, and will not always allow for the data in the existing system to be easily, rapidly and accurately transferred. Therefore, within the software industry, there is a built-in inertia which causes the software user to consider long and hard before moving from one software package to a rival. The idea of having the existing package maintained, upgraded and improved is much the most attractive option.

11.4   Categories of software maintenance

Following Sommerville (1989), we make the following definitions or descriptors for software maintenance:

- *Perfective maintenance* is the term given to the work on a piece of software which improves the program without actually correcting any specific bug. So, for example, perfective maintenance could be improving the user interface by making it easier for the user to perform common steps in the system, or producing a predefined report format for a weekly sales report which would otherwise have to be redefined each week. It is estimated that perfective maintenance accounts for approximately 65% of total maintenance costs.
- *Adaptive maintenance* is the term used to describe changes in the programs which are made necessary in order to suit changes in the requirements of the users. Thus, when tax regulations change and new sections of an accounts program have to be written, or when a different printer needs to be installed, the changes to the program fall into this category. Adaptive maintenance is estimated to account for something like 18% of total maintenance costs.
- *Corrective maintenance* is the correction of actual errors. Sometimes the errors are actual bugs in the programs; at other times it could be a problem with the design, or even the specification. Corrective maintenance accounts for something like 17% of total maintenance costs.

11.5   How can software engineering help the software maintenance process?

As may be observed from the preceding discussion, the key to successful software maintenance is a clear understanding of the existing software, a clear understanding of the requirements and a simple approach to making changes. In theory, at least, software engineering methods can contribute to each of these.

11.5.1   The software specification

The first contribution is the clear specification for the software. In the software specification document, the objectives of the client are made clear, as are the specific requirements of the system. This helps the software maintainence engineers to understand the type of change which needs to be made, and identifies how fundamental the change is likely to be. For example, changes which add an additional objective or two, but where the additional objectives are consistent with the original aims of the software, are likely to be less problematic than are changes where the new objectives are at odds with the original aims.

The thoroughness with which the software specification is undertaken should, in theory at least, mean that the number of changes which will be needed subsequently should be kept to a minimum. As we have seen earlier in this book, the more possible changes to the software which can be foreseen when the software is initially specified and designed, the more likely it is that opportunities for modification can be built into the programs at the design stage.

One of the features of the software specification which is particularly significant, is the consideration of those qualities of software which we described as *non-functional* requirements, since these often form the basis of *perfective maintenance*. Since these requirements are considered in a well-run software engineering project from the beginning, it is possible that a significant part of the largest maintenance component could be saved.

11.5.2   The software design

The software design builds upon the software specification. Therefore the issues identified in the preceding paragraph are important here too. In particular, if likely changes in requirements have been included in the specification, then provision should be built into the design for these changes to be made without serious problem.

11.5.3   The program structure

Part of the program design dictates how the programs should be structured. Structured programs are easier to maintain than unstructured programs, because it is likely that maintenance tasks can be completed through the rewriting and exchange of *sections* of code. Since each particular procedure has precise specifications for its input, processing and output, it should be a relatively simple matter to rewrite a small number of specific procedures so that they continue to behave as before, but exhibit specific additional functions or qualities (Figure 11.1).

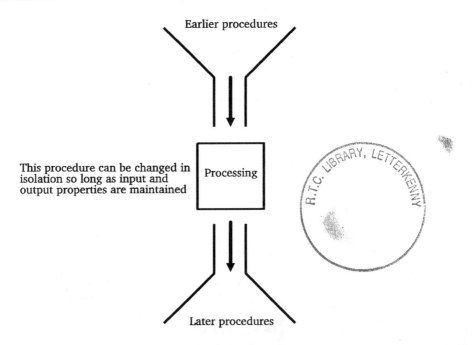

Earlier procedures

This procedure can be changed in isolation so long as input and output properties are maintained

Processing

Later procedures

Figure 11.1 Structured programs may be maintained by rewriting individual procedures

11.5.4 The program quality

Program quality is hard to measure (see Chapter 12) but nevertheless, well-engineered programs are deemed to be of higher quality than others. Thorough testing, a good structure and clear objectives are three features of good quality programs and all are of significance in program maintenance. Particularly important is the thorough and accurate testing of the code, which can reduce the cost of corrective maintenance to almost nil. Naturally, this is one of the motives for the use of formal methods and provably correct programming (see Appendix I).

11.5.5 The system documentation

The perennial complaint about existing programs made by program maintainers is that the documentation which accompanies them is inadequate, incomplete or absent. We have identified the writing of good documentation as being a key feature of software engineering, and the rigorous nature of the software development process should enable some structure to be imposed on the documentation. This in turn should help the software maintenance engineer.

One problem with poorly documented code is that there may be an obvious

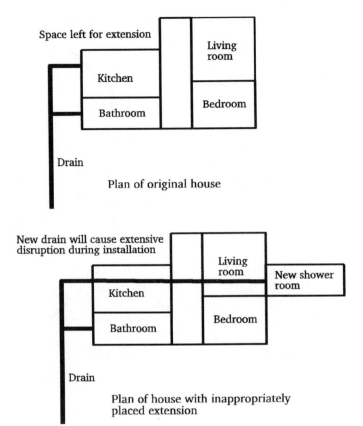

Figure 11.2 An extension can be added to a house most satisfactorily if provision was made for it when the house was built

way of making particular modifications to a program and this may be ignored in the maintenance process. For example, the original developers might foresee likely changes in the requirements, and build in a way of adding the necessary procedures. If this is not documented, then it could be that the software maintainers will add the new procedures in a less appropriate way. Figure 11.2 demonstrates the comparable situation for adding an extension to a house.

The documentation of maintenance is another important factor. It is important that a completely revised document which takes account of changes through maintenance should be produced. This should highlight changes to the requirements, changes to the specification and design and changes to the programs themselves. The failure to document maintenance changes thoroughly can result in serious problems with subsequent maintenance.

11.6   Factors affecting software maintenance costs

Software maintenance costs are influenced by a number of factors. Naturally, one of the critical factors is the *quality* of the software originally developed. We shall consider this in a little more detail in Chapter 12. Other factors include:

- The program life: Programs which were expected to have a short life may be less well engineered than those expected to be kept for a long time. Sometimes programs are kept for much longer than intended and obviously this can cause increased maintenance costs. In other cases, programs kept over a long period are likely to need more adaptive maintenance because the underlying requirements will change over time. This can be as a result of changes in the hardware, or changes in external requirements. It is also fair to say that users will demand enhanced user friendliness from programs with a long expected life.
- The stability of staff: When programs are maintained by the team who created them there are a number of cost savings. The team is likely to be familiar both with the specification, and with the methods of implementation used. Therefore the time taken to become familiar with the existing package will be less and it is more likely that new procedures written will mesh satisfactorily with the old. The feeling of *ownership* of the original programs can be an added benefit.
- The application: Some programs are more important than others and demand greater standards of performance. For example, a program monitoring the intensive care unit in a hospital should be of higher reliability than one running a payroll, although both applications are important. The precise requirements of the application will determine how soon after a minor problem has arisen it will be necessary to rewrite the programs.
- Hardware stability: The less frequently the underlying hardware is changed, the less often the programs need to be changed to match.
- Dependence on external factors: The less often factors influencing the specification change, the less frequently the software will need to change to reflect this.

11.7   Exercises

1. Talk to the users of a particular system and draw up a list of maintenance requirements. Distinguish the requirements as perfective, corrective or adaptive maintenance.
2. Consider whether the software maintenance process which you investigated in question 1 should be undertaken. Compare the likely costs and benefits. Would it be preferable to develop a completely new system?

Chapter 12

Software quality assurance

12.1 Introduction

The principal theme of this book has been the development of software of high quality through the introduction of improvements in the *processes* which make up the software development cycle. Therefore we have been discussing the two issues of:

- Developing quality software
- High-quality development of software.

In this chapter, we shall pull together some of the ideas about quality software and quality development, and attempt to answer the question: How might you measure the quality of software?

12.2 What is quality software?

It is easy to look around the computer industry and identify examples of low-quality software. Almost every user seems to be able to relate examples of a program which either did not work, gave the incorrect answer to some problem or crashed catastrophically in use, taking lots of work, effort and often data with it. This basic understanding of bad software gives us a natural basis for beginning to make a definition of good software:

Good software is:

- Correct, in that it performs to its specification
- Reliable, in that the accuracy of the answer can be predicted consistently
- Robust, so that it will not suddenly fail for no good reason.

As we discussed in earlier chapters, however, there is more to it than that. Programs need to suit the *users*, by being user friendly. Programs need to suit the *owners* by being flexible, portable and maintainable. Programs need to be *efficient*, whether that means that they operate quickly, use little memory or computer time or need few operators. All of this demonstrates that software quality is a very complex issue, and it is a naive computer scientist who declares that program X is a higher quality product than program Y without qualification of what the word *quality* means.

We would like to be able to measure the quality of software. For example, it would be useful to be able to come up with a grading scheme whereby each software package could be given a score, out of 1000, say, which would enable us to distinguish its quality from its rivals. Unfortunately no such scheme is in existence, and it would be impossible to devise a scheme which could be universally accepted, since the range of priorities of different potential users of a single package can be widely different.

For example, some users of a database package may be particularly concerned to produce large amounts of output quickly. For them the speed of the operation will be paramount, and it could be that user-friendliness can be sacrificed in favour of speed. Other users of the same package may want to use it with vast numbers of operators with minimum training. For these users, user friendliness could be far more important than speed. To judge the package according to both criteria could give a misleading picture to both groups of potential users.

Thus it is appropriate to adopt a variety of different ways of measuring software quality. In the next section we introduce some of those which are most satisfactorily calculated.

12.3 How can software quality be measured?

Precise measures of software quality, where they are possible, are known as software quality metrics. Sommerville (1989) identifies four *reliability metrics*:

- *Probability of failure on demand* measures the proportion of occasions when the software fails to provide the service which is demanded of it. For safety critical systems, such as health monitoring, guided missile control or process control, this can be a very useful measure of software reliability, since the proportion of failures to provide the required service determines the rate of failure of the system. Where failures are catastrophic, the failure rate is the most significant statistic.
- *The rate of fault occurrence* measures the number of faults which arise in a fixed time period. This is a generally useful reliability measure.
- *Mean time between failures* (MTBF) or *mean time to a failure* (MTTF) records the average period which will elapse for the system before the next failure. This is a standard measure of hardware reliability.
- *Availability* measures the proportion of the time when the system is operating and offering a service. This is quite a useful measure, because it takes into

account the time taken to correct faults and restore the system to operational condition rather than just the number of faults detected.

As we can observe already, the problem of making accurate, reliable and meaningful measurements of the reliability of software depends upon the adoption of a satisfactory metric. For reliability, this is possible.

We can also introduce meaningful measures of speed, through the use of *benchmarking*. Here rival software solutions to a problem are subjected to timed trials. The times taken for each solution are then combined in an appropriate and agreed way to give a score for the software performance. These scores are described as the benchmark performances of the different software solutions.

Even software benchmarking faces problems. Schneider and Bruell (1991) point out that it is important to distinguish the performance of the program as written, from the theoretical performance of an implemented algorithm. For example, it could be that an efficient algorithm is implemented by an inexperienced programmer and therefore executes more slowly than would an inefficient algorithm which has been programmed by an expert. Thus we must be careful to distinguish between the *actual* performance of a computer program and the *theoretical* performance of the algorithm.

But if software benchmarking can be problemmatic, it is impossible even to begin to quantify some of the other qualities of software. How do we attach a score to the user-friendliness of a program, or to its ease of maintenance? Even if we found a way to assign a score, it would have to take into account the subjective nature of the assessment. Some users like graphical user interfaces (GUIs) such as Microsoft Windows, others do not. Some users like to be able to make small modifications frequently, others restrict maintenance to major overhauls. Software may suit one particular type of use better than another.

So precise measurement of software quality may be a utopian ideal rather than a reality. It could be that we need to restrict our measurements to those qualities which permit measurement, and that we should pursue other ways of ensuring that software produced is of high quality. After all, just because we measure quality we cannot assume that we can deliver it, and conversely we may be able to deliver high quality which is recognisable even if it is not quantifiable!

12.4   What is quality software development?

One approach to the delivery of high-quality software, and the one which this book has as its focus, is the desire to improve software quality by controlling more closely the software development process. The argument is based upon the idea that a rigorous software development process leads to improvements in the quality of the output, and most definitely improves the confidence which we might have in its quality.

In Chapter 2, we described some aspects of the quality debate in our outline of some of the ideas which underlie BS 5750. The desire to *know* how high is the quality of the output of a system must become a focus for the attempts to improve quality.

So quality software development involves careful control over the processes and an adherence by the software developers to the chosen rigorous framework which imposes the control. The very fact that a software engineering approach is adopted, whether based upon the specific methods described in earlier chapters, or more generally in a way which adopts alternative methods, the approach allows the generation of the quality software we desire. The adoption of good management strategies for control is crucial and therefore we turn to consideration of project management.

12.5   Management for quality

The ideas of project management have been mentioned at several points within this book. We have seen the importance of project management tools in helping to plan the stages in software development, and we have seen how they can be used to help *cost* a software development process. But project management is a much wider area of activity than simply planning the interrelationship of the stages in the project. In this section we identify some of the issues and refer the interested reader to more detailed references, such as Sommerville (1989).

Software project management is difficult for many of the same reasons that software quality measurement is difficult. The product of the software development process is intangible, still a new process viewed with suspicion and not widely understood, and has a reputation for maverick developers. Against this background, there is great demand for good quality software, many millions of pounds are expended each year on software development and the future of the developed world depends on good quality computer software. Therefore the stakes in software project management could hardly be higher.

Projects need to be managed so that they are accurately costed, planned and scheduled. The project needs to be monitored and reviewed at regular intervals. This last point is probably the most important feature in computer software development, because mismanagement of one type or another is where many failures of software developers to deliver to deadlines, to deliver a reliable product or to deliver at all, have their roots.

When a project has been underfunded, when deadlines have been set too soon, when the developers have been subject to insufficient supervision, we have the prime causes of poor quality output. Management of software projects needs to be undertaken by people who understand the nature of the work, rather than by those frightened of it. This is demonstrated again and again in the history of computer software development. Where the management have been in full control of the developments, high-quality products have been delivered at a good price and on time.

On the other hand, where projects have been costed unrealistically to win contracts, when deadlines are forced unrealistically early, and when the project managers ignore the advice of software developers that more time is needed in testing, there is a recipe for disaster. Software project management is crucially important, and is an underutilised area of activity.

12.6   Verification, validation and testing

Some of the most important processes by which software quality is assured come under the title of validation, verification and testing. The software specification document is a key to determining the quality of a software solution to a problem.

It provides a focus for us to consider:

1. Whether the needs of the client have been correctly identified
2. Whether the software being implemented satisfies the objectives of the client
3. Whether the software has been produced to a high quality.

We need to be careful to distinguish between:

- Failure of the specification to meet the requirements of the client
- Failure of the software engineer to provide a system which meets the specification.

Corresponding to these potential problems, we identify two corresponding techniques:

- Requirements validation: checking that the specification is correct. In other words, checking that the product we are making, if correctly made, is the right product for the client.
- Software verification: checking that the software produced is a faithful implementation of the requirements specified. This is an assessment of the quality of the implementation.

The methods used to check the quality of the software produced usually revolve around methods of testing. As part of the implementation phase of a project, testing is a critical activity (see Chapter 10).

12.6.1   Requirements validation

Requirements validation is concerned with the problem of checking that the software produced has been be designed to perform the job required. In a sense, this corresponds to the market research phase in the design and development of any new product. The market researchers conduct their survey and determine that there is a market for a particular car provided that it seats six adults, and therefore the definition of the requirements given to the design engineers specifies that the new design must seat six. Correspondingly, in a software development project, the systems analysts are responsible for the initial investigations which determine what the user requires. It is part of this responsibility for the analyst to ensure that the requirements of the user are validated against the requirements definition from which the software engineer constructs the specification. Requirements validation addresses the question, are we making the right product?

Requirements validation often relies upon the experience of the systems analysts, who are able to bring previous project knowledge to bear upon the present situation and thereby recognise likely gaps in the definitions. Unfortunately, it is in the nature of this sort of exercise that every project has sufficient uniqueness to make it likely that something may be missed.

The real problem with requirements validation stems from the fact that clients will often only realise their particular need for a specific feature in a new system when they are able to experience working with the system. This can typically mean that changes in the requirements arise at the very last minute and cannot be built into the design in the way which would be desirable. One possible way around this is to produce an early prototype version of the system, possibly through the use of a CASE tool, or through employing some other software prototyping device. This can help in the early identification of problems in the software specification. As we shall see, the provision of good requirements specification methods can be a key to the provision of rapid, worthwhile and accurate prototyping (Figures 12.1 and 12.2).

12.6.2   Software verification

The second part of the quality control associated with the requirements specification is known as *software verification*. Here we are concerned with checking that the software produced conforms to its specification. In other words, we are concerned to check the quality of production of the software.

Since the requirements definition and specification form the basis from which the software engineer works, these documents can provide a good basis for checking on the quality and accuracy of the software implementation. As we shall see later in this book, using these documents to check on the quality of software written can be fraught with difficulties, but it is nevertheless the most appropriate place to begin.

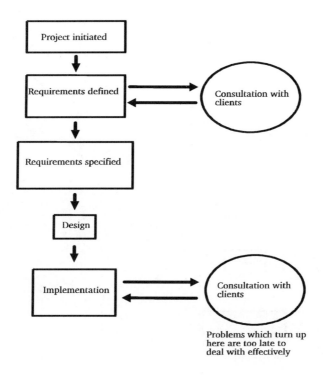

Figure 12.1 Requirements validation

12.7 Software tools and software quality

We have described elsewhere the specific ways in which software tools can contribute towards software testing and quality assurance, and how project management tools can help in the setting of realistic targets and costing for a programming project.

But tools are no substitute for expertise or experience. Nor can project management tools replace appropriate personnel applying appropriate controls to the software development process. The use of software tools within the development process is just one way in which software quality can be assured. But quality software development needs more than just rigid observance of a set of rules, and more than just a rigorous quality assurance system. Quality software development requires a commitment by all involved in the development process to ensure that the product is of the highest possible quality.

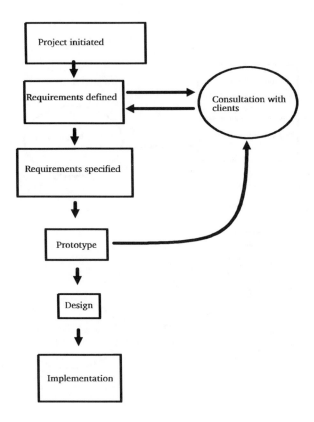

Figure 12.2 Requirements validation with prototyping

12.8   Exercises

1. Choose a piece of software with which you are familiar and assess its quality. Consider each of the relevant aspects of quality and make a list of the improvements (if any) you would desire in an upgrade.

2. For the dentist's appointment computer system, what particular qualities in software would you desire? Can you suggest ways of measuring the quality of rival products?

3. For any software tools with which you are familiar, list the functions provided which contribute explicitly to quality control. Can you identify further implicit quality control features within the software tool which are important?

4. To what extent do you believe that project management techniques could contribute to *your* successful writing of computer software?

Chapter 13

Software engineering: alternative approaches

13.1 Introduction

In this final chapter, we consider several issues which are important in software engineering and we raise some important questions:

1. How can software engineering be used for small projects?
2. What techniques are appropriate in the development of *new* systems?
3. How will software engineering need to change in the future?

13.2 Software engineering and small projects

Software engineering is a marvellous theory. The desire to improve the quality of software produced and to enhance reliability and reduce costs in the long run can be accepted without question. And yet, when faced with small projects, software engineering methods can appear cumbersome and unnecessary.

The software engineering cycle, as we have described it, is ideally suited to the development of large computer-based systems which will be used over a long period to perform important processing tasks. These systems are operated at enormous expense, by large numbers of staff and have a significant developmental budget.

But not all software is of this nature. Many software users are small businesses or departments within a larger company who need access to computer programs. They also require that the programs should be of high quality, but the budget for the production of the software must be much smaller, and therefore the software engineering process as we have described it may be too expensive and cumbersome.

Other software may be of a very different nature. In scientific investigations, for example, programs are often written and run once or twice in order to find the answer to a particular problem. Again, it is important that the programs written must be of high quality in order to ensure the reliability of the answers which they give. However, these programs must often be developed quickly and inexpensively to test out ideas, and the detailed processes of software engineering can seem largely irrelevant.

From this discussion we have identified several characteristics of small projects. They may be:

- Constrained by a tight budget
- Used in an organisation which does not employ computer experts
- Required to be developed quickly
- Used only a few times.

The problem for us is to reach some sort of compromise between, on the one hand, the software engineering techniques which will provide reliability but at significant cost in terms of money and delayed completion, and, on the other hand, the much quicker, less expensive, but potentially dangerous approach which ignores rigorous methods in the quest for expediency.

Within any project, we can identify the stages which software engineering follows as:

1. Decide what is needed
2. Describe what is needed
3. Determine how it should be provided
4. Develop the programs
5. Review the performance of the completed system.

These five stages can be seen as an irreducible minimum, and any attempt to develop software in a way which misses out one or more of these stages is in danger of disaster. For small projects, it is therefore appropriate to consider whether there are suitable ways of cutting the costs and time involved in each stage.

One way in which users of small systems can save time and money is to use a packaged solution if one is available. We saw this in Chapter 9 as a potential implementation strategy for any system, and it has clear advantages for small systems. Even where no suitable package appears to be marketed, it can be worthwhile investigating other organisations with similar requirements to see whether it might be possible to acquire programs already developed for somebody else.

Even if a packaged solution is not available, it is worth considering carefully the ways in which other users have coped in similar circumstances. It is dangerous to be an innovator in computing, since new ideas do not always work quickly or effectively. For small users, the advice to play safe and adopt a known strategy is suitable, even if rather unexciting.

It is also important to realise that time spent in developing, documenting and optimising programs needs to be balanced against the time saved in running them later. For programs which have a limited life, with no likelihood of future adaptation, it should be possible to keep development costs down by concentrating on *functional* parts of the program and not on on the user interface and documentation.

The other important factor when considering small systems is *people*. In large organisations, the people who will be using the computer software are often remote from the developers, and there are all sorts of complicated strategies which can be employed to make the users more involved in the system development process. For small systems, this is rather different, because the users of the system are typically very closely involved with the decision to develop software and use it for a specific purpose. Therefore many of the problems which a small organisation may face because of limited resources can be balanced by a greater involvement and commitment among those who will use the system.

13.3   Development of new systems

Software engineering has grown out of systems analysis, which itself developed from earlier methods of improving system reliability and efficiency. Thus, there is an underlying assumption built into the process that we will begin with an existing system of some kind and we will try to improve it. There is also the underlying belief that *computerisation* is the key to improving most existing manual systems.

This means that the software engineer faces a problem when trying to apply conventional methods to developing completely **new** systems.

One way of looking at the software engineering method which we have considered in this book, is to consider a succession of four types of data-flow diagrams.

We begin with the **current physical** diagram. This demonstrates the ways in which things are done at present.

By thinking carefully about what is actually being done, rather than the ways in which it happens, the current physical diagram can be developed into a **current logical** diagram.

The contents of the current logical diagram can then be considered against the needs and aspirations of the users. This allows the unnecessary parts of the current logical diagram to be removed and new demands inserted. The **required logical** diagram is produced.

Finally, knowing from the required logical diagram exactly *what* is required, we can consider *how* it is to be provided, and this is demonstrated in the **required physical** diagram.

The discussion above is simplified, but nevertheless indicates the key part played in systems development by reaching an understanding of the existing ways of doing things as a method for determining what would be the requirements of a new system.

There are two specific types of project where this approach falls down. Clearly projects which do not develop from an existing system are one problem area. Here there are several approaches which can be taken:

- Sometimes the absence of an existing system is not significant, because there may be similar existing systems in use in other places. In this case the design can be based upon other systems.
- Sometimes the new system has been commissioned with the express intention of trailblazing a new approach. In this case, the absence of any existing system is replaced by the availability of clearly defined aims and objectives for the system development.
- Sometimes, if a system is completely new, it will be necessary to determine some ideas at the outset and build a prototype system as quickly as possible to provide a basis for further discussion and decision.

Another problem area can be those projects which develop from an existing system which has major failings. Here it can be best to begin by throwing away the existing system and working as if there had been no previous system in existence. The problem with this can be that some methodologies are rigid in their demand that we begin from an existing system if one exists. Gane and Sarson (see, for example, Gane 1990) take the view that a decision must be taken with each new system development as to whether the models should be based upon an existing system or developed from scratch. This *flexible* view is one with which we would agree.

13.4   Software engineering and the future

Software engineering has developed a long way since it first appeared. However, most mainstream software engineering projects are concerned with conventional approaches to software development through the use of high-level computer programming languages.

In Chapter 9, we showed that the use of conventional programming is just one way of implementing computer systems and, while it may be the most flexible way, it can also be the most expensive and least reliable. Therefore one trend which we believe will gain pace in future software engineering is the development of methods better suited to the analysis and design of systems, which will be most naturally implemented using an alternative strategy, such as through an applications package. It seems likely that methods which more nearly suit these developments will also help in providing software engineering approaches for smaller projects.

Other developments in software engineering and related areas are likely to reflect changing views of the ways in which programs are developed and organisations are managed. We describe ETHICS and object-oriented programming in the Appendices. Here we have faced a real problem, because we have not been able to integrate these ideas fully into our treatment of the material. The problem is this: one of the chief concerns of software engineers is to avoid implementational dependence. However, the very methods of software engineering as we have described them pre-suppose certain ways of managing change, and certain ways of solving problems. Therefore, within all that we have described, there is an underlying philosophy which predisposes us to particular conclusions. Object-oriented programming should not be thought of as *a way to write a program* which has been thought through in a conventional way. ETHICS and other human-centred approaches to analysis lead to completely different ideas again. It could well be that these different approaches to systems development will need to be integrated within a broader field where methods can be selected to suit the needs of particular projects.

Appendix I Formal Methods

Introduction

In this appendix, we will consider how formal methods, an idea introduced in Chapter 7, are used in simple practical cases. The examples and approach used in this chapter closely follow the material in Ford and Ford (1993) to which we refer the interested reader for a more detailed discussion.

The principal features of formal methods

We have seen already that a formal method attempts to remove the ambiguity and improve the clarity of descriptions offered by informal methods of specification. Such informal methods are typically based upon natural languages, such as English. We also aim to retain the implementation independence of the description, which would be lost if we used a specification based upon one of the well-structured computer languages, such as Pascal or ADA.

We identify the following principal features of a formal specification:

1. A formal specification makes clear the nature of all the objects to which it refers
2. Objects may be defined in terms of other objects
3. The amount of intuition required to understand the specification is eliminated in theory at least. Intuition needed to understand the specification may be kept to a minimum in some practical cases.

As soon as we begin to try to make formal specifications, we shall experience the following problems, which need to be set alongside the strengths which we desire:

1. Formal methods can be clumsy and tedious to use. It can be that some of the statements seem to state the obvious in a very unclear way.

157

2. However careful we are, we shall always end up defining some entities in terms of others which we have not defined. It is therefore important that we accept some *fundamental* categories to form the basis for other definitions

3. We need to be particularly careful with the use of natural language in a formal definition. Terms are used to mean what we have defined them to mean. They no longer have their *intuitive* meaning

4. Some people find a formal definition harder to understand than an informal one. Perhaps this is simply a reflection of the common misuses of language which people make in their speech.

Becoming more formal

The use of formal methods in software specification is becoming more widespread in practical cases now, but is still a comparative innovation. As a result, many of the methods and publications on the subject have their roots within research conducted by computer scientists rather than in actual practical applications. A number of different techniques and approaches have been developed, and for the purposes of the illustrations in this appendix, we have chosen to discuss the Vienna Development Method (VDM).

Hekmatpour and Ince (1988) give the following description of the steps involved in VDM:

- Specify the system formally
- Prove that the specification is consistent
- **Do**
    - refine and decompose the specification (i.e. produce a *realisation* of the specification)
    - prove that the realisation satisfies the previous specification
- **Until** the realisation is as concrete as a program
- Revise the above steps.

This sequence gives us a much more focused view of the objectives of our formal approach. Certainly the use of a formal specification does allow us to give a clear and unambiguous statement of the functional requirements of our system, but there is more to it than that. The nature of the formal specification allows us to transform the specification as written into the statements of a programming language.

But what exactly are the benefits of this transformation?

One of the principal problems tackled by the software engineer is the software verification. We met this term in Chapter 7, and it refers to the methods of ensuring that the program as written does indeed satisfy its specification. The conventional way of verifying software involves the testing of the programs in different ways. For example we have met the ideas of top-down testing, bottom-up testing, equivalence partitioning and so on.

Unfortunately, without an unambiguous specification, it is not possible to test the software rigorously to ensure it meets the specification. In addition, we have identified fundamental problems with the success of software testing. Therefore a different approach to software verification, based upon the use of a formal specification, would be attractive.

The VDM method for developing software adopts the following strategy. Instead of completing the software development, then trying to experiment with different test data to see whether the system performs to specification, as in the usual software development cycle, VDM defines a process whereby each section of the program is *proved* to be correct, because it is developed in a formal and *provable* way from the original specification. Thus, at every stage in the development process, the current specification is decomposed into subspecifications which are then *proved* to be equivalent to the original.

In this way, the system can be **proved** to be correct as specified, rather than just demonstrated to work correctly for a particular set of test inputs. In theory, at least, systems developed in this way can be expected to be totally foolproof and to display very high accuracy and quality.

The problem, naturally, is the question of how we go about proving that specifications are equivalent, one with another, and that requires some discussion of what is meant by the word *proof*. Many books on formal methods begin with a discussion of logic and mathematics before introducing their purpose in terms of program development. This is unfortunate, because it can mean that some computer scientists never appreciate how formal methods can help in their work.

In order to begin to appreciate the fundamental difference between a *proof* and a *test*, we shall consider a very simple mathematical equation:

$$2x + 3 = 5$$

Most of you will no doubt be able to solve this mathematically, the sequence of operations goes something like this:

- $2x + 3 = 5$
- Subtract 3 from each side
- $2x = 2$
- Divide each side by 2
- $x = 1$

These steps in the solution of the equation form the basis of a *proof* that if $2x + 3 = 5$, then $x = 1$. In other words, we are certain after following these steps that the **only** solution of the equation is $x = 1$, so long as we can be sure that the rules of elementary algebra can be trusted!

On the other hand, we might have tried to reason as follows:

- Look at the equation $2x + 3 = 5$
- Try $x = 1$ - success! so $x = 1$ is a solution
- Try $x = 2$, $x = 3$, etc. No others work
- Conclude $x = 1$ is the only solution.

This second 'method' is one which is doomed to failure in general, but happens to succeed in getting the right answer this time! People who understand mathematics would make the following criticisms of the trial and error method:

1. We have looked only at a few positive whole numbers, we do not know whether we should also be looking at fractions, negative numbers or very large numbers as alternative answers.
2. We might have found an answer. But is it **the** answer, or are there in fact lots of answers we have not found? This second method fails to give a satisfactory account of this.

Testing of computer software may not be quite as naive as the trial and error method of solving the equation, but it lays itself open to just the same criticisms. We only test the performance of the software against the inputs where we *predict* that there will be an interesting outcome. We make no attempt to *prove* that the output at non-tested inputs is acceptable.

If we now look in some more detail at the simple mathematical example which we have just discussed, we see that it begins with a specification of a condition: in other words we begin by saying, What we are looking for is a suitable value of x which will satisfy the equation $2x + 3 = 5$. At this point in the discussion, we are not concerned with how one might go about actually finding the value of x which we seek, but rather we are interested in *defining* what conditions the sought for value will satisfy when we find it. The series of steps which we have identified then illustrates how we could go about realising our aim and finding the value of x.

In a moment, we shall look at a simple formal definition of a *function*. By analogy with the approach just described, here too we begin by making a clear statement of exactly how the function which we require will behave: we will give careful consideration to the questions of:

- what are the requirements on the *parameters* on which the function acts, known as the *preconditions*?
- what are the requirements when the function is completed, known as the *postconditions*?

Once we have a clear idea of these preconditions and postconditions, we will then be in a position to know exactly what the function must be able to do. It is from this *implicit* description of the function that we must work to give the *realisation* of the function in its explicit form. In other words, we aim to finish up with a clear-cut series of instructions which go to make up the function. These instructions should be provably equivalent to the pre- and post-conditions specified.

Example

In order to keep things as simple as possible, we shall define a very simple mathematical function which multiplies odd integers by 2 and divides even integers by 2. The function is not defined for non-integers.

We shall begin by posing three questions:

1. What does the function do? To be precise, what sort of things does it act upon (what is its *domain*) and what sort of answers does it give (what is its *codomain*)?
2. What are the preconditions, if any?
3. What are the postconditions, if any?

For the present, we shall call our function f, and we shall answer the questions in order:

1. f is a function defined on those real numbers which are integers and it gives an answer which is a real number (and happens also to be an integer). We shall consider f as a function from real numbers to real numbers. This is written as follows:

$$f(x : \text{real})y : \text{real}$$

In other words, the function f takes as its input the value x which is a real number and gives as output the value y which is also a real number.

2. The precondition for the function f is that the real number x must be an integer. We shall express this in the form:

$$PRE\ x \in Z$$

which uses some shorthand notation, notably the Z to represent the set of all integers (whole numbers) and the symbol $\in$ to represent the words *is a member of.*

3. Finally, we need to give the postcondition, which says that if x is odd then $y = 2 \times x$ and if x is even then $y = x/2$. Again we have a special way of writing this down:

$$POST\ \{(x \text{ even}) \wedge (y = x/2)\} \vee \{(x \text{ odd}) \wedge (y = 2 \times x)\}$$

The special symbols used here are $\wedge$ for **and** and $\vee$ for **or**. We may therefore read the formal statement in the following way: 'POST condition: either x is even and $y = x/2$ or x is odd and $y = 2 \times x$'

This implicit specification looks as though it is rather long-winded, but this is really only because we are trying to understand what is going on as we write it down. In practice, the formal specification of the function f in the above form would simply say:

$$f(x : \mathrm{real})y : \mathrm{real}$$

$$PRE\ x \in Z$$

$$POST\ \{x\ \mathrm{even} \wedge (y = x/2)\} \vee \{x\ \mathrm{odd} \wedge (y = 2 \times x)\}$$

To work from this formal definition of the function f to a *realisation* of the function f (i.e. a description of how it might be implemented), we shall need to show that:

For every real number x which satisfies the precondition for f, the value y output by f satisfies the postcondition

In other words, to prove that we have realised the function f in its formal specification, it will be **insufficient** to consider simply some appropriate test data and work on the basis that if f tests accurately, then it must be accurate. Instead, we shall aim to *prove* that the realisation of f satisfies its specification exactly.

Before we attempt to complete this proof, look again at the statement of the proof required. This statement makes explicit the role of the precondition when it comes to the realisation of the function. For the proof is concerned *only with those values of x which satisfy the precondition*. For any value of x which does not satisfy the precondition of f, we have no information specifying the output, y.

To begin with, we present an explicit realisation of the function f:

$$f(x)\underline{\Delta}\ \mathrm{if}\ x\ \mathrm{even\ then}\ x/2\ \mathrm{else}\ x \times 2.$$

To prove that this expression for f is indeed a realisation of the specification, we proceed as follows:

1. $x \in Z$ (precondition)
2. x is even or x is odd (property of Z)
3. **from** x is even (case 1)

    (a) $y = x/2$ (specification)

    (b) **infer** if x is even then $y = x/2$

4. **from** x is odd (Case 2)

    (a) $y = 2 \times x$ (Specification)

5. **infer** if x is even the $y = x/2$ else $y = x \times 2$

This proves that the given realisation is valid.

Example

We shall now consider a second mathematical example of a formal specification. This time, we will work more directly to the specification, then prove that we have an appropriate realisation of the given specification.

Define the function M by the following:

$M(x : \text{real})y : \text{real}$
PRE: True
POST: $\{(y = x) \vee (y = -x)\} \wedge (y \geq 0)$

Notice here how the precondition is 'True' which implies that the specification must hold for all real values of x.

We claim that the following definition of $M(x)$ gives a valid realisation of this specification:

$M(x) \underline{\Delta}$ if $x > 0$ then x else $-x$

and we proceed to prove this:

Proof:

1. $x \in R$
2. $x > 0$ or $x \leq 0$
3. $\{(y = x) \vee (y = -x)\} \wedge \{y \geq 0\}$
4. **from** $x > 0$

    (a) $\{(y = x) \wedge (y \geq 0)\} \vee \{(y = -x) \wedge (y \geq 0)\}$

    (b) $\{(y = x) \wedge (y \geq 0)\} \vee \{False\}$

    (c) **Infer** $(y = x)$

5. **from** $x \leq 0$

    (a) $\{(y = x) \wedge (y \geq 0)\} \vee \{(y = -x) \wedge (y \geq 0)\}$

    (b) $\{False\} \vee \{(y = -x) \wedge (y \geq 0)\}$

    (c) **Infer** $(y = -x)$

6. If $x > 0$ then $y = x$ else $y = -x$

Example

Having looked at two mathematical examples of formal specification, we shall now consider an example drawn from data processing. The example will, of necessity, be a straightforward one, but illustrate how the methods which we have just met might be applied in practice.

This example is concerned with a Bank ATM cash dispenser machine. These machines will be familiar to many readers. Bank customers use a plastic card which has a magnetic identification strip attached to it. This card is inserted into the machine and the customer types in a personal identification number (PIN). The cash dispenser machine checks with the stored PIN number list to ensure that the correct number has been entered to match the inserted card before either giving a menu of options or rejecting the customer as an imposter.

Here we will consider the function which the machine uses to distinguish between a real customer and an imposter. We will start with an informal description of the function, then proceed first to a formal specification (which is implicit) and finally to a proof that the implicit representation can lead to an explicit realisation.

Informally, we will consider the function *Truecustomer* to take a plastic card and a PIN number and determine whether the entered PIN number identifies the user of the card as the true customer of the bank.

We shall write our formal specification as follows:

Truecustomer (x:plastic card, y:PIN number) z:{True,False}
PRE: x belongs to correct bank
POST: $\{\text{match}(x,y) \wedge (z = \text{True})\} \vee \{(\text{not match}(x,y)) \wedge (z = \text{False})\}$

Notice how these specifications depend upon a function *match* already having been set up. This function *match* is assumed to give a *true* value if the card x and the PIN number y are compatible and a false value otherwise. We will not at this stage attempt a formal specification of the function *match*.

A possible realisation of the function *Truecustomer* could be expressed as follows:

Truecustomer(x,y) $\triangleq$ if match(x,y) then true else false.

The proof that this realisation is satisfactory is straightforward:

1. x = plastic card, y = PIN number
2. (match(x,y) = true) $\vee$ (match(x,y) = false)
3. **from** match(x,y) = true

   (a) (match(x,y) = true) $\wedge$ (z = true)

   (b) **infer** if match(x,y) = true then z = true

4. **from** match(x,y) = false

   (a) (match(x,y) = false) $\wedge$ (z = false)

   (b) **infer** if match(x,y) = false then z = false

5. (if match(x,y) = true then z = true) $\wedge$ (if match(x,y) = false then z = false)
6. if match(x,y) = true then true else false

which completes the proof.

Exercises

1. Define the function Square as follows:

   Square(x:real) y:real
   PRE: True
   POST: $y = x^2$

   Prove that the following is a valid realisation of this function:
   Square(x) $\underline{\Delta}$ $x \times x$

2. Define the function Sign as follows:

   Sign(x:real)y : $\{+1, -1\}$
   PRE: $x \neq 0$
   POST:$\{(x > 0) \wedge (y = +1)\} \vee \{(x < 0) \wedge (y = -1)\}$

   Prove that the following is a direct definition of the sign function:
   Sign(x) $\underline{\Delta}$ if $x > 0$ then $+1$ else -1.

3. Here is a specification for the (real) square root function *Root*:

   Root(x:Real)y:Real
   PRE: $x \geq 0$
   POST: $(y^2 = x) \wedge (y \geq 0)$

   Why do we need the precondition in this case?
   Prove that the following is a valid explicit form for the function *root*:
   Root(x) $\underline{\Delta} + \sqrt{x}$

4. Here is a specification for the function which checks the catalogue in a library for a book required:

   Search(Searchitem:Title, Catalogue:List of books):Result:{True,False}
   PRE: True
   POST: $\{$(Searchitem $\in$ Catalogue)
   $\wedge$ (Result $=$ True)$\} \vee \{$(Searchitem $\notin$ Catalogue) $\wedge$ (Result $=$ False)$\}$

   Prove the validity of the following realisation of this function:

   Search(x,y) $\underline{\Delta}$ if x $\in$ y then **True** else **False**.

Appendix II ETHICS

Introduction

This appendix outlines a very different approach to finding and describing a user's requirements. As we saw in Chapter 4, SSADM is a highly structured method for conducting a systems analysis, and an increasing number of computer scientists recognise the value of alternative strategies such as the one described here.

What is ETHICS?

Effective technical and human implementation of computer-based systems (ETHICS) has been developed by Enid Mumford for over 15 years (see Mumford and Weir 1979). ETHICS covers the whole of the system life cycle, but concentrates on the analysis and design stages.

ETHICS, as the name suggests, has an explicitly stated philosophy based around the socio-technical and participative approaches. ETHICS promotes the workforce as being central to organisational change, their contentment being a key factor in the overall success of the project. It also adopts a holistic approach to system development, considering the issues involved rather than the processes and data. It is interesting to note that ETHICS developed out of the social sciences and consequently the people involved in the system:

The socio-technical approach is defined by Mumford (1983b) as:

> One which recognises the interaction of technology and people and produces work systems which are both technically efficient and have social characteristics which lead to high job satisfaction.

Job satisfaction is defined according to the following criteria:

- Are the skills and knowledge of the employee being utilised and developed? There are two perspectives which need to be considered when establishing the goodness of this fit: that of the employee and of the organisation. These views may differ. For example a machine operator may be quite content operating the same machine all the time, but the organisation may believe operating a variety of machines could benefit the company more. In this type of situation a process of discussion and negotiation might be necessary. These types of discussions are key to the operation of ETHICS.
- Does the job fit the employee's qualifications, age, background and so on? We all have perceptions about the type of person we are and the jobs which would be suitable for us. In time of recession, well-qualified people often get posts which are inappropriate for them because there is nothing else available. This situation is likely to lead to a disaffected workforce.
- The tasks carried out must fully exercise the employee and give a sense of achievement. When new systems are being developed, particularly computer-based systems, this element is often disregarded, with previously interesting jobs becoming repetitive and mundane.
- For an organisation to be really successful, the employer and the workforce should have a shared value system. This is clearly true in service-based organisations such as colleges and hospitals, but it is also true in business. One example of a company with a successful ethical fit is the Co-operative Bank, whose mission statement includes the following statement:

> To act as a caring and responsible employer encouraging the development and training of all our staff and encourage commitment and pride in each other and the group. To develop a close affinity with organisations which promote fellowship between workers, customers, members and employers. To be a responsible member of society by promoting an environment where the needs of local communities can be met now and in the future. To be non-partisan in all social, political, racial and religious matters. To act at all times with honesty and integrity and within legislative and regulatory requirements. (Co-operative Bank 1993)

The staff are expected to be in sympathy with this viewpoint and the bank has a distinctive image which is claimed to give it a unique position in the market place.

It should be noted that a marketing organisation might have a shared belief in the importance of making money - ethical fit does not always have to be based on ideology!

The second philosophical strand is *participation*. In ETHICS, all the relevant groups of people are consulted. An open systems approach is taken to this, with parties outside of the system boundary also being consulted. Thus a warehouse wanting to improve its record keeping would consult the suppliers and consumers of the product, as well as the employees who are going to operate the new system. The view taken in ETHICS is that change often results in conflict, some of this resulting from difficulties involving the various job *fits* described above. Participation is a useful tool for allowing these difficulties to be discussed and compromises to be found. The different types of participation were described above. There are other considerations which need to be taken into account when implementing participation in ETHICS:

1. For participation to be successful, the participants need to be aware of all the relevant information. This requires a degree of openness on the part of management.
2. Participation is usually based around a design group which makes the major decisions concerning the choice of equipment, the allocation of responsibilities and so on. The composition of this group is vital, as it must be representative of all the interested groups.

Central to both of these issues is staff training: the participants will require training in the operation of their own company and also in the techniques necessary for the analysis and design tasks. The latter training is usually carried out by systems analysts within the group.

The manner in which ETHICS is implemented varies according to the source. The following is a brief resume of the major steps:

1. Why Change? It is not assumed that change is good by definition and so the design group is required to produce a statement supporting the need for change.
2. System Boundaries. The relevant systems are identified and the manner in which they impact upon one another considered.
3. Description of Existing System. This is a specification of the current operation of the system. It is mainly carried out in order to educate the members of the design team.
4. Definition of Key Objectives and Tasks. These result from an analysis of the existing system. The different areas within the organisation are considered and objectives are specified as appropriate.
5. Diagnosis of Efficiency Needs. Shortcomings within the existing system are identified. Some of these may be unavoidable, but others will be overcome in the new system.
6. Diagnosis of Job Satisfaction Needs. At this stage, the job satisfaction issues (the *fits* mentioned earlier) are discussed and negotiated over.
7. Future Analysis. The design group tries to anticipate future developments · in order to make the new system as flexible as possible.
8. Specifying and Weighting Efficiency and Job Satisfaction Needs and Objectives. In this stage all the objectives already identified are drawn together and prioritised.

9. The Organisational Design of the New System. The different ways in which the organisation can be altered in order to meet some or all of these objectives are identified. These solutions are then ordered according to their desirability.

10. Technical Options. The technical solutions, which tie in with the possible organisational changes, are also considered. Different hardware and software will be evaluated.

11. The Preparation of a Detailed Work Design. The chosen solution: both the organisational and technical details are designed in detail.

12. Implementation. The design group coordinates the implementation of the new system, planning and organising the change-over and so on.

13. Evaluation. The new system is evaluated to see how well it meets the agreed objectives. This may result in the whole process being started again.

It can be seen from this description that throughout the system development process, the needs of the organisation and of the individual employees are primary, and the technical aspects are secondary. Also very little consideration is given to the details of the implementation. Thus any programming would need to be carried out using separate techniques, such as those used in the software engineering cycle.

It is easy to see that the focus in ETHICS is on understanding rather than on rigorous application of techniques. Therefore the methods used are informal, such as interviewing, discussions and observation. Software tools have little part to play.

Appendix III Object-oriented methods

Introduction

We have met on several occasions within this book the notion of an *object-oriented* approach to problem solving. In this appendix, we describe the approach in a little more detail and encourage the interested reader to pursue the topic through further reading. We have found the introduction to object-oriented methods in Pinson and Wiener (1988) very useful, and we would refer interested readers to this book.

Adopting object-oriented methods

Object-oriented programming relies upon a completely different approach to problem solving and software design. Thus we talk about object-oriented methods, rather than object-oriented programming, and in order to adopt an object-oriented approach to solving a problem, software engineers need to take a decision to work in an object-oriented way from the start.

Structured approaches to program design and development in conventional high-level procedural languages involve describing the steps involved in undertaking the necessary processing in terms of standard instructions within the language. In other words, the language itself is seen to provide basic building blocks. Procedures and functions are built up using these blocks to make more complex processes. In other words, the processing which we want to undertake in the program has to be moulded to fit in with the built-in features of the language.

Similarly, procedural programming requires that data structures are built up from known structures provided by the language. Proponents of the object-oriented approach would argue that closer examination of procedural language solutions to many problems reveals an unnatural and uncomfortable series of compromises between the way people might naturally think about a problem, and the way the computer-based solution has, of necessity, been constructed.

Object-oriented approaches try to get away from the straitjacket of procedural languages to give program developers the scope to describe solutions and problems in a more natural way. It is claimed that the approach can enhance reliability and improve maintainability of the software produced, and so it is attractive to all those concerned with improving the quality of software. Over recent years, wider availability of programming media which support object-oriented methods has led to a growth in interest in these methods. An object-oriented approach provides a natural basis for a different description of software engineering methods.

The principal features of object-oriented methods

Object-oriented approaches to problem solving are concerned with *sending messages to objects*. Pinson and Wiener (1988) describe the four steps in an object-oriented approach as:

1. Stating the problem
2. Identifying the objects in a solution
3. Identifying messages to which those objects should respond
4. Establishing a sequence of messages to the objects that provide a solution to the stated problem.

Clearly, when we look at this list, we see hints of precisely those issues which we have found important throughout this work. Software engineers must begin by coming up with a very clear description of the problem which they must solve. In some sense, the objects defined correspond to the data structures built up within the data dictionary, and the messages to be communicated have a certain parallel with procedures which have to be designed and written. However to describe the process of object-oriented problem solving purely in this way is to lose sight of its specific features. These are the properties of objects known as:

1. Abstraction
2. Encapsulation
3. Inheritance
4. Polymorphism.

Abstraction and encapsulation

One of the problems about the world is that it is too complex to describe adequately. An approach to overcoming this problem is by becoming more *abstract* and describing the way some *idealised* system behaves. Obviously, in order to be of any practical use to us, the idealised (and simplified) system has to bear appropriate resemblance to the world which it describes. The hope is that, by gaining a greater understanding of the behaviour of the abstraction, we shall gain a corresponding understanding of the world which it provides a model of.

Abstraction in object-oriented programming provides an exactly parallel function. In order to solve a particular problem which relates to the real world, we really need to gain sufficient understanding of the world to be able to describe it. This is one reason why programming in a conventional procedural language can be seen as rather hard, since the programmer is faced with a system model which is too complex and therefore the program seems impossible to write. However, the idea of creating an abstract object which behaves in a restricted class of ways we can describe adequately, can make the task much simpler.

Objects are defined in terms of the properties which they have, the features which they display and the messages which they respond to. Their properties, features and message responses are each abstractions of the real world, and the objects are said to *encapsulate* the abstractions.

Inheritance

In normal communication, it is often convenient to describe one thing as being similar to another. In the same way, objects may be described in terms of other objects from which they *inherit* some of their features. We sometimes describe this in terms of a hierarchical structure rather like a family tree, in which objects at each level inherit properties from those at a higher level, but where each object may possess private properties which are unique to itself or shared with objects at lower levels.

Polymorphism

One problem common to many programming languages is that particular functions and procedures have to relate specifically to the context in which they are used. Thus, if a procedure called *output* is to be used to print name and address labels, we would not be able to use the *output* procedure to print out a party guest list. The idea behind polymorphism is that this type of problem should be overcome.

Different kinds of *objects* can have associated with them particular processes which are interpreted *in the context of* the object under consideration. Thus, it would be considered quite possible that a *print* command might have a particular meaning when it relates to an object which consists of a name and address, with a rather different meaning when it relates to a payslip. This contextual interpretation of processes is both natural and convenient.

Object-oriented approaches: the future

Interest in object-oriented programming has grown significantly as the range of available programming systems has widened. It is now possible to use object-oriented programming methods within programs developed using C++ or (Turbo) Pascal, and neither hardware nor software costs need constrain the developments. The potential benefits claimed for object-oriented approaches are substantial and merit serious consideration. However conservatism within the computer industry and the significant rethinking of project development at the earliest stages if object-oriented methods are to be adopted is likely to slow down its adoption more widely.

Appendix IV Software prototyping

Introduction

In this appendix, we meet the idea of prototyping software solutions to problems. We begin the discussion by considering why software prototyping is an attractive proposition, and we identify some general issues which arise when considering prototyping. Finally, we outline several approaches to software prototyping. The content of this appendix is based upon material from Ford and Ford (1993).

What is prototype software?

In mechanical engineering, the term prototype is used to refer to a preproduction model of a proposed new product. When the product actually goes into production, many will be built and so a few prototype models are made so that the performance and features of the prototypes can be tested and any changes in design can be made before mass production is commenced. Prototype cars, for example, will cost considerably more to build than a production vehicle, but the savings made by making changes to the design before production commences are enormous.

Software to solve individual problems is not normally mass produced. While the aim is still to use a prototype to help inform the design process, it is essential that the prototype software should be cheaply and quickly produced. Therefore prototyping in software engineering is slightly different from conventional engineering prototyping, since the performance of the prototype may not be as good as performance of the final version, and this may be a deliberate choice.

The following list of features of prototype software is adapted from a list given by Hekmatpour and Ince (1988):

- It is a system which works and not just a drawing or design
- It may be a throw-away model of the actual system, or a first step in an

evolutionary approach to systems development

- It must be built quickly and cheaply
- It is part of a development process which includes evaluation and modification.

Why prototype software?

One of the important aspects of software quality control is the validation of requirements. In other words, we have to ask whether the definitions and specifications of the software to be developed are appropriate for the task in hand; that is, are we building the right product?

Making sure that the specification faithfully demonstrates the requirements of the client is the fundamental role of systems analysts in the investigation process, but inevitably their clients often find it hard to describe in words just what their needs are. No simpler is the problem of looking at the written specifications drawn up by the analysts or software engineers and seeing whether the technical description matches the users' needs. The clients or users understand what the programs should look like and how they should perform, but diagrams and text describing the specification can be almost meaningless.

Therefore it can be helpful to provide the users or clients with an early prototype system which exhibits many of the features of the specified system in order that the system can be tried out and problems with the specification can be identified at this early stage. The problem is, *How do we produce a prototype system at high speed and minimum cost?*

Elementary software prototyping

Exactly how difficult it is to develop prototypes is dependent upon the nature of the project. For projects which are 'standard', it may be possible to produce a prototype with relative ease, whereas for a more individual project, prototyping may be more difficult.

Applications package-based programming

Some standard software can assist the prototyping process. Therefore, when software is developed using a standard package, such as a database package, it may be possible for a naive system to be established very rapidly and then refined to the user's particular needs. This later refinement takes the time in development terms, and makes the program really satisfactory in use. This early and unrefined version can give the client an idea of the 'feel' of the software.

Programming based on high-level language: use of libraries

High-level language programmers are becoming increasingly aware of the need to
store and reuse parts of programs which are widely applicable. Therefore new
programs may be developed by using procedures originally written to perform the
same tasks in other applications. The procedures are added to a library of routines
available for reuse. As with the use of software applications packages to speed up
the development process, reuse of code can be a very great asset in producing a
rapid example system, even if the library procedures do not perform exactly like
the specification. As in the previous case, the important thing about a prototype
is that it helps the client to think through exactly what should have been specified
in the first place.

A similar approach uses bought-in standard library routines which are commercially available for developing programs. These share many of the advantages of
reusing program code, while also giving a wider variety of facilities than any individual programmer would be likely to have developed and a guarantee of quality
and reliability from the supplier. These techniques are particularly encouraged
when programs are to be developed using a high level language which promotes
the use of library facilities (such as C or Modula-2) (see Ford 1990 for further
details).

Program generators

There are a number of specialised 'program generators' available which will write
programs automatically. Typically they use a questionnaire approach to determine
the answers to a series of questions about the application and then to write the
actual code. In theory at least, the programs developed in this way could be
used *live* and so the idea behind these program generators is attractive, but they
tend to be rather less satisfactory in practice than the advertising might suggest.
In particular, their area of applications tends to be rather limited, since they
can usually generate efficiently programs of a particular type. Their efficiency
in generating programs which are actually usable is questionable, but they are
nevertheless valuable in the production of prototypes and the prototype programs
can sometimes be recoded to give the final versions.

Screen generators

A method which uses screen generation software can be attractive. This software
allows for the design of input and output screen to be completed without any of
the processing of data being implemented. Clearly it is somewhat quicker and
easier than other prototyping methods, since it ignores the question of processing
which has to happen in a particular program, and concentrates instead upon the

user interface. Users typically have a good understanding of the data requirements of a system and the values which they would expect to have to input, and of the forms of output which they would be likely to need. Therefore the use of screen generators is a very much simplified approach to prototyping ,since we produce the forms of input and output and give the users the opportunity to comment upon the result. This is the cheapest, but the least reliable form of prototyping.

CASE tools

Some CASE tools include a code generation option which allows a specification recorded by the CASE tool to be quickly translated into a program in a suitable language. Often programs developed in this way do not run efficiently, but for users with access to a suitable CASE tool, this can be a relatively inexpensive and rapid way of developing a prototype package.

The cost of prototyping

One of the arguments which can be levelled against the use of software prototyping is expense. This argument may not be true, but it is very difficult to provide a convincing reason to explain why not!

The argument against prototyping is based upon the following:

1. Under the throw-it-away prototype system the development of a prototype is an additional stage in the software development process which is otherwise unnecessary. Therefore the conclusion is that it is wasteful.
2. Prototyping may not really be very much faster than developing the system itself, and if the prototyping medium is very different, as in the case of prototyping languages such as EPROL, then the work involved in producing the prototype will save no time in developing the final system.
3. Prototyping delays the start of implementation of the final system. In an industry where delays in the delivery of completed software projects is a major problem, introducing a clear cause of additional delay is unattractive.

Arguments which may be made in favour of prototyping are as follows:

1. Prototyping improves the completeness and accuracy of the specification of the program. Therefore the final result may be of higher quality than otherwise.
2. If the specification is more accurate, then the amount of time spent on maintenance may be reduced. This should be set against the generally accepted statistic that between 50 and 80% of software costs arise out of maintenance of the software. If we are able to reduce this time wasted, then there will be clear cost savings.

3. Staff can be trained and can provide early evaluation of a new system using the prototype. It can be that the actual live running of the system can actually commence at an earlier date, because staff training can be completed before the program is really ready.

4. Prototype systems which are completely functional can be used. Therefore it might be possible to offer a client the availability of a low specification working system at an early date, with the completed and fully functional system following later when it is complete.

5. Prototype systems do not necessarily need to be thrown away and therefore time spent on their development is not necessarily wasted. Evolutionary prototyping is one example where prototyping forms an integral part of the development of a system.

As can be seen from these arguments for and against prototyping, the problem of persuading clients of the wisdom of prototyping is that the potential gains from its use, while possibly great, are intangible. On the other hand, the costs of prototyping are immediately clear. Furthermore, the occasions when prototypes yield the greatest gains in the software development process, are the occasions when the initial design has a major flaw. But these are the occasions when the initial prototype is rejected by the client and a second prototype needs to be produced. Therefore the greatest gains from prototyping happen when the use of the prototype seems to cause even greater cost!

Bibliography

Abrial J.R. (1980) *The specification language Z,* Oxford University Programming
Research Group

Avison D.E., Fitzgerald G. (1988) *Information Systems Development: Methodologies, Techniques and Tools,* Blackwell Scientific Publications

Benyon D., Skidmore S. (1987) Towards a toolkit for the systems analyst, *The Computer Journal* **30** No. 1, 2-7

Checkland P. (1990) *Systems Thinking, Systems Practice,* John Wiley and Son

Codd E.F. (1970) A relational model of data for large shared data banks, *Communications of the ACM,* **13** 377-387

Computing (1992) Issue on CASE and CAST Tools, September 24th 1992.

Co-operative Bank (1993) *Current Accounts,* Co-operative Bank, Manchester.

Cutts G. (1991) *Structured Systems Analysis and Design Methodology,* Blackwell
Scientific Publications

Flynn P. (1992) *A dental system,* Unpublished Project, Anglia Polytechnic University

Ford N.J. (1990) *Computer Programming Languages: A Comparative Introduction,* Ellis Horwood

Ford N.J., Ford J.M. (1993) *Introducing Formal Methods: A Less Mathematical Approach,* Ellis Horwood

Gane C. (1990) *Computer Aided Software Engineering,* Prentice Hall

Gane C., Sarson T. (1979) *Structured Systems Analysis: Tools and Techniques,*
Prentice Hall

Hekmatpour S., Ince D. (1988) *Software Prototyping, Formal Methods and VDM,*
Addison Wesley

Jackson M.A. (1983) *Systems Development,* Prentice Hall

Jayaratna N. (1986) Normative information model-based systems analysis and design: A framework for understanding and evaluating methodologies, *Journal of Applied Systems Analysis* **13** 73-87

Jones C.B. (1990) *Systematic Software Development using VDM (2nd edn)*, Prentice Hall

Longworth G., Nicholls D. (1986) *SSADM Manual, Vol 1: Tasks and Terms*, NCC Publications

Mumford E. (1983a) *Designing Participatively*, Manchester Business School

Mumford E. (1983b) *Designing Human Systems*, Manchester Business School

Mumford E., Weir M. (1979) *Computer Systems in Work Design-the ETHICS Method*, Associated Business Press

Nicholls D. (1987) *Introducing SSADM: The NCC Guide*, NCC Publications

Pinson L.J., Wiener R.S. (1988) *An Introduction to Object-Oriented Programming and Smalltalk*, Addison Wesley

Pressman R.S. (1987) *Software Engineering: A practitioner's approach*, McGraw-Hill

Schneider G.M., Bruell S.C. (1991) *Concepts in Data Structures and Software Development*, West Publishing

Skidmore S., Wroe B. (1988) *Introducing Systems Analysis*, NCC Publications

Sommerville I. (1989) *Software Engineering (3rd edn)*, Addison Wesley

STARTS Guide, National Computing Centre

Index